Installation Ceremonies for Every Group

OKS ... for living life well!

26 Memorable Ways to Install New Officers

PAT HINES

Brighton Publications

Copyright © 1997 by Pat Hines

Brighton Publications, Inc.
P.O. Box 120706
St. Paul, MN 55112-0706
612-636-2220

First Edition: 1997

Library of Congress Cataloging-in-Publications Data
Hines, Pat,
      Installation ceremonies for every group : 26 memorable ways to install new officers / by Pat Hines. —1st ed.
         p.   cm.
      Includes bibliographical references and index.
      1. Societies—Miscellanea. 2. Associations, institutions, etc.—Miscellanea. 3. Rites and ceremonies. I. Title.
HS35.H56   1997   96-40273
367' .068—dc21   CIP

ISBN 0-918420-31-8

Printed in the United States of America

Table of Contents

Introduction / 5

Building Blocks (toy blocks) / 7

Broadway Beat (Broadway songs) / 12

Let There Be Light (candles) / 17

Sweet Time (candy bars) / 21

Chain Reaction (chains) / 25

Rainbow (colors) / 29

The Best Deal (deck of cards) / 34

Give a Hoot (endangered species) / 39

New Bouquet (flowers) / 43

Fruitful Future (fruit) / 48

Laugh Time (gag tokens) / 53

Sparkle Plenty (gems) / 57

A Pinch Will Do You (herbs) / 62

Hallelujah (religious songs) / 67

Puzzle Pieces (jigsaw puzzle) / 72

Key Capers (keys) / 76

Flying High (kites) / 80

Grand Opening (letter openers) / 84

Best Seller (parts of a book) / 88

It Is Written (pens) / 93

Quotables (quotations) / 97

Grand Gourmet (recipes) / 102

The Good Book (scripture quotations) / 106

Stepping Out (shoes) / 110

Terrific Tokens (tokens) / 115

Branching Out (trees) / 119

Gift Index / 125

Organization Index / 125

Bibliography / 126

Introduction

Over the years, I have been asked to be the installing officer for many different organizations. Desiring to have meaningful ceremonies, I found that there were very few resource books available that contained installation services. As a result, I generally ended up writing most of the ones that I used.

This book contains twenty-six of my installation ceremonies, ranging from lighthearted to serious. Each ceremony's chapter contains appropriate gift suggestions, amount of preparation required, approximate running time, and suggested groups for which the ceremony could be used. From my experience, installing officers are not always members of the club for which they have been asked to conduct the ceremony. Therefore, the directions and suggestions listed for the following ceremonies should make any installation easy to do.

The officers installed in these services generally include treasurer, corresponding secretary, secretary, second vice-president, first vice-president, and president. There is one ceremony that does not include the office of corresponding secretary. In these ceremonies, the second vice-president is listed as the head of the program committee, and the first vice-president is the membership chairman. Even though tasks are assigned to specific officers in these services, the duties of the officers should be changed to fit the needs of a club.

Flexibility is the key to success for any ceremony. Because each organization is unique in its set of officers and their responsibilities, it is necessary to check the organization's by-laws before the ceremony and make additions or deletions accordingly. The officers' duties, as listed in the club's by-laws, should be the ones included in the ceremony.

Organizations exist in great numbers in America, ranging from church groups to community service clubs. In most cases, these groups install officers on a regular basis. From one installing officer to another, it is my hope that one of these ceremonies will meet your needs, and that this book will become a valuable resource to you and your organization.

Building Blocks

This ceremony uses blocks to illustrate how officers and members of an organization must work together to accomplish club goals. Every block is needed in a structure, and every member is needed in a club. The officers of an organization provide important leadership. They are an integral part of the group's framework, similar to the support blocks at the bottom of a building. If one block is removed from a building, the structure can come tumbling down. Likewise, if one officer fails to perform her duties, the club's success is in jeopardy.

As a memento of the event, give each officer an alphabet block. If possible, use blocks that have the initials of each office. Choose a "T" for treasurer, a "C" for corresponding secretary, an "S" for secretary, an "S" for second vice-president, an "F" for first vice-president, and a "P" for president. New blocks can be purchased at a toy store or a discount department store. Second-hand blocks, still in good condition, can also be used. Go to garage sales, flea markets, thrift stores, and rummage sales to locate them. Preparation includes the time needed to find and buy the necessary blocks. It will probably take less time to buy new blocks than second-hand ones. Cost is minimal since alphabet blocks, new or used, should be fairly inexpensive.

Another alternative is to give each officer one block from a set of multi-shaped, multi-colored building blocks. Because each officer's duties are different, each officer should be given a different block. These can be found at the same locations as the alphabet blocks. If this gift suggestion is used, time is needed to locate and buy the blocks. New building blocks generally cost more than the alphabet blocks.

You might give each officer a plexiglass block that has been personalized with the person's name and office. These blocks can be ordered from stationers or catalogs. Time is a definite factor with this suggestion, so do not wait until the last minute. This idea will be more high-priced than the other two.

This ceremony is about 15 minutes. Appropriate for any club, this theme would lend itself well for any educational organization since these groups are in the business of building for the future and cultivating the imagination of students. Prepare the script and purchase the necessary blocks in advance. Script preparation includes obtaining the new officers' names since they are used in the ceremony. Also, inform the officers that they will be required to answer an installation question with the words, "I do."

INSTALLATION CEREMONY

One gift most young children receive early in life is a set of blocks. Blocks fuel imagination, and children can spend hours building houses, skyscrapers, and cities with them. Children learn quickly that every block in their created structures is essential. If one block is removed, the building can come tumbling down. Likewise, every member in a club is vital to the well-being of an organization. If one member falters, a group is weakened.

Officers are a significant part of the framework in a club. Just as the blocks at the bottom of a structure support an entire building, an organization's officers support their club when they provide competent leadership. When officers perform their specific tasks, the club structure remains strong.

Tonight, the officers of the _____ (name of club) shall be installed using a theme of blocks. The blocks given are symbolic reminders to the officers that they are now an integral part of this club's framework. The successful completion of their duties will help keep their club intact. Will the newly elected officers please come forward? (Have the officers line up in order with the treasurer first.)

————————#————————

_____ (name of treasurer), as treasurer, you are the cornerstone of this club. As the cornerstone is the basic element of a structure, you are a necessary element of your club. Your duties include collecting and depositing money, paying club bills as directed by the executive board, and giving a monthly financial statement to your club. Do you promise to fulfill the many duties of your new office? (Officer should answer, "I do." Pick up officer's block.) You have publicly declared that you will help to keep your club's framework intact. May this block be your constant reminder. (Give the block to the officer.)

————————#————————

_____ (name of corresponding secretary), as corresponding secretary, you are the arch of this club. As the arch is a graceful span of an opening in a structure, you, through your writing, represent your club in a graceful manner. Your duties include writing letters and taking care of all of your club's correspondence. Do you promise to fulfill the many duties of your new office? (Officer should answer, "I do." Pick up officer's block.) You have publicly declared that you will help to keep your club's framework intact. May this block be your constant reminder. (Give the block to the officer.)

————————#————————

_____ (name of secretary), as secretary, you are a buttress of this club. As the buttress supports and gives stability to a building, you support your club with accurate records. Your duties include listening attentively at all times, writing up the minutes of each meeting, and keeping the history of the club. Do you promise to fulfill the many duties of your new office? (Officer should answer, "I do." Pick up officer's block.) You have publicly declared that you will help to keep your club's framework intact. May this block be your constant reminder. (Give the block to the officer.)

—————————#—————————

_____ (name of second vice-president), as second vice-president, you are the lintel of this club. As a horizontal lintel spans and carries the load above an opening, you reach out to the interests of the members and support this year's programs. Your duties include chairing the program committee, learning about all club matters, and assisting your president. Do you promise to fulfill the many duties of your new office? (Officer should answer, "I do." Pick up officer's block.) You have publicly declared that you will help to keep your club's framework intact. May this block be your constant reminder. (Give the block to the officer.)

—————————#—————————

_____ (name of first vice-president), as first vice-president, you are the pillar of this club. As a pillar provides firm upright support for a super structure, you provide strength to this club. Your duties include chairing the membership committee, keeping all club members informed as to club business, learning about club policies and procedures, and working closely with your president. Do you promise to fulfill the many duties of your new office? (Officer should answer, "I do." Pick up officer's block.) You have publicly declared that you will help to keep your club's framework intact. May this block be your constant reminder. (Give the block to the officer.)

—————————#—————————

_____ (name of president), as president, you are the facade of this club. As the front of a building, or facade, is given special architectural treatment, you take on a special dignity representing your club. Your duties include presiding at all meetings, appointing committees and chairmen, following up on all club matters, and representing your organization at all times. Do you promise to fulfill the many duties of your new office? (Officer should answer, "I do." Pick up officer's block.) You have publicly declared that you will help to keep your club's framework intact. May this block be your constant reminder. (Give the block to the officer.)

(To the membership.) Members, you are the rest of the elements in this club's structure. Each one of you has different skills and talents that are needed by this organization. Use your many abilities and support your officers. When you work together, you can build a strong club from top to bottom and accomplish great things. Keep your club's framework solid.

Broadway Beat

An important part of life, music has been known to calm nerves, evoke emotions, and inspire dreams. Broadway musicals have contributed greatly to the genre of inspirational music. The titles of specific songs of encouragement are the perfect setting for the installation of a club's officers. Within a club, the officers are a calming and guiding force. The fulfillment of their respective duties provides leadership and helps an organization attain its goals.

You might give each officer a copy of the specific song used in their induction ceremony. Sheet music can be purchased at any music store. It might need to be ordered, so start looking for the songs months in advance of the ceremony. Do not make photocopies of music sheets. To do so is a copyright infringement and illegal. The titles used in the ceremony include "Over the Rainbow" from The Wizard of Oz, "Put on a Happy Face" from Bye, Bye Birdie, "Getting to Know You" from The King and I, "The Impossible Dream" from Man of La Mancha, "You'll Never Walk Alone" from Carousel, and "Climb Ev'ry Mountain" from The Sound of Music. Because of the high cost of sheet music, this idea could be quite expensive. However, the only preparation required is obtaining the copies of the music.

Another gift option is to buy each officer a cassette tape that has Broadway songs on it. If possible, try to find the specific songs used in the ceremony. Those songs are listed above. If you cannot locate all of those songs, a tape that has a collection of Broadway hits would be fine. Go to record stores and discount department stores in your search for the right tapes. It might take some time to find the tapes, so do not procrastinate if you choose this gift suggestion. Cassettes can vary in price from moderate to high.

A third possibility is to give each officer a potted plant, or flower, that has some musical-designed ribbon in it. A symbolic gift, the ribbon represents the musical aspect of the ceremony. Potted plants, or flowers, can be found at greenhouses, florist shops, or discount department stores. Craft stores, fabric stores, and florist shops carry many styles and sizes of ribbon. Make florist bows with the ribbon and then adorn each plant with one bow. If you do not have time to make six bows, ribbon streamers can be used to decorate the plants, or flowers. This option requires time to purchase the plants and ribbon, and to make the bows, or streamers; however, it has the advantage of being reasonable in cost.

This ceremony is between 10 and 15 minutes in length and is best suited for an organization, such as a musical society or theatrical group. Make certain that the gifts and script are ready prior to the day of the installation. Preparation of the script includes obtaining the new officers' names since they are used in the ceremony.

INSTALLATION CEREMONY

In all of our lives, music can generally be heard daily. We are so accustomed to hearing it, that, at times, we do not even know it is softly playing in the background. Melodies have been known to soothe troubled brows, stir emotions, and provide inspiration.

Officers of an organization are also called to calm, stir, or inspire members. The fulfillment of their various duties is often done so quietly that members are unaware of how their club runs so smoothly. Efficient leaders contribute greatly to the well-being of their club. They provide direction and guidance necessary for the achievement of club goals.

Tonight, each officer of the _____ (name of club) will be installed to the accompaniment of a famous Broadway song. The titles, which symbolize the duties of each officer, are meant to inspire the officers to reach to new heights. Will the newly elected officers please come forward? (Have the officers line up in order with the treasurer first.)

When we think of a rainbow, thoughts of a pot of gold often come to mind. _____ (name of treasurer), as the newly elected treasurer, you will be handling your club's pot of gold. Your duties include depositing money, collecting dues, writing checks, and giving monthly financial statements to your organization.

"Over the Rainbow" from The Wizard of Oz is the song that symbolizes your office. As you assume your new duties, may you find your rainbow and see your dreams fulfilled. (Give the gift to the officer.)

—————#—————

If you want to present a good public image, what better way than with a happy face. _____ (name of corresponding secretary), as the newly elected corresponding secretary, you will be handling your club's public image. Your duties include answering letters, writing notes to members, and communicating happiness to everyone.

"Put on a Happy Face" from Bye, Bye Birdie is the song that symbolizes your office. As you assume your new duties, may you find it easy to smile and make others smile with you. (Give the gift to the officer.)

—————#—————

Who knows us better than someone who knows our history? _____ (name of secretary), as the newly elected secretary, you are the keeper of your club's history. Your duties include taking minutes at every meeting and recording the actions of your organization for the future. Your club's history is in your care.

"Getting to Know You" from The King and I is the song that symbolizes your office. As you assume your new duties, may your minutes become easier to write as you get to know your club better. (Give the gift to the officer.)

————————#————————

Selecting programs that will interest all members may seem like an impossibility. _____ (name of second vice-president), as the newly elected second vice-president, you are the program chairman for your club. Your duties include working with the program committee and assisting the president when needed. Since you are now in a position of leadership training, you must also familiarize yourself with your club's by-laws.

"The Impossible Dream" from Man of La Mancha is the song that symbolizes your office. As you assume your new duties, may you find the strength to meet all the incredible challenges of your position. (Give the gift to the officer.)

————————#————————

As a part of a group, club members must never feel alone. _____ (name of first vice-president), as the newly elected first vice-president, you are the membership chairman for your organization. Your duties include helping all members feel needed and wanted. Keep enthusiasm high, recruit new members, and retain old members. As understudy to the president, you must know your club's by-laws, policies, and procedures.

"You'll Never Walk Alone" from Carousel is the song that symbolizes your office. As you assume your new duties, may your walk be filled with courage, hope, and faith. (Give the gift to the officer.)

————————#————————

When we think of a mountain, thoughts of something lofty and high come to mind. _____ (name of president), as the newly elected president, you have been given your club's highest honor. Your duties include presiding at meetings, appointing committees and chairmen, encouraging members, and following up on club matters to make certain that they are being done properly and on time.

"Climb Ev'ry Mountain" from The Sound of Music is the song that symbolizes your office. As you assume your new duties, pursue your dreams until they become realities. May this year be a mountain climbing experience for you. (Give the gift to the officer.)

(To the membership.) Members, you can be heard as the other songs that make this club complete. Your various skills and abilities are vital to this organization. With your support and encouragement, your club can realize all of its dreams and goals. Working together, you can create an organization that is filled with perfect harmony.

Let There Be Light

This ceremony uses candles to symbolize how the officers of an organization light the way for the membership. A candle needs to be lit in order to bring light to a darkened area. Likewise, club officers need to fulfill their specific duties in order to bring success to an organization. Just as a candle gives off light to help lead the way, the officers provide guidance and direction to the membership.

A keepsake for each officer would be a candle that is to be lit during the ceremony. Use tapered candles that are at least 10 inches in length. They can be a variety of colors, or all the same color. Candles can be purchased at a gift shop, a department store, or a discount department store. A larger white candle, at least 6 inches in width, will also be needed. As the officers are installed, they will light their candles from this candle which symbolizes the club. The candles can be decorated with a ribbon tied around them. The ribbon, no wider than one-half inch, should be a color that complements the candles, or use ribbon colors that are representative of the club. Ribbon can be purchased at a craft store, or at a florist's. The preparation time for this suggestion will include going to the store to buy the candles and ribbon, and then tying the ribbon onto the candles. This gift idea is relatively low in price.

The ceremony will last about 10 minutes. It is a solemn ceremony that could be used for any women's organization, particularly civic and religious groups. Have the script and candles prepared prior to the day of the installation. Do not forget to take matches with you.

Before the meeting begins, place the larger white candle in the middle of a table with the matches beside it, and the other candles around it. Prior to the ceremony, inform the new officers that they will be lighting a candle from the center white candle. The officers also need to know that they will be required to answer an installation question with the words, "I do."

INSTALLATION CEREMONY

Since ancient times, candles have been an important source of light. When burning, candles provide light to an area and can show the way to someone who is lost. Likewise, the officers being installed tonight are an important source of club leadership. They provide guidance and direction for the membership.

(Light the large center candle.) This candle represents your organization, the _____ (name of club). The officers will light their individual candles from this central one. In so doing, they are making a promise to this club that they will fulfill their tasks and be a light to the membership. Will the newly elected officers please come forward? (Have the officers line up in order with the treasurer first.)

The treasurer of an organization takes care of the club's finances. You will collect dues, pay bills, and give an accurate financial statement at each club meeting. Do you accept this new responsibility? (The officer should answer, "I do.")

(Give the officer a candle to light from the central one. Once it is lit, continue.) In lighting this candle, you have agreed to fulfill your obligations to your club. May you be a financial light to this membership.

————————#————————

The corresponding secretary of an organization takes care of the club's correspondence. You will write necessary letters being prompt and courteous at all times. Do you accept this new responsibility? (The officer should answer, "I do.")

(Give the officer a candle to light from the central one. Once it is lit, continue.) In lighting this candle, you have agreed to fulfill your obligations to your club. May you be a social light to this membership.

The secretary of an organization takes care of the club's records. You will write up the minutes of every meeting, keeping an accurate account of all actions taken by your group. Your minutes become an important part of your club's history. Do you accept this new responsibility? (The officer should answer, "I do.")

(Give the officer a candle to light from the central one. Once it is lit, continue.) In lighting this candle, you have agreed to fulfill your obligations to your club. May you be a recording light to this membership.

The second vice-president of an organization chairs the program committee. Provide guidance to this committee so that a variety of programs are selected for a diverse membership. In this office you will also receive valuable leadership training as you acquaint yourself with your club's policies and procedures. Do you accept this new responsibility? (The officer should answer, "I do.")

(Give the officer a candle to light from the central one. Once it is lit, continue.) In lighting this candle, you have agreed to fulfill your obligations to your club. May you be a programming light to this membership.

————#————

The first vice-president of an organization chairs the membership committee. You must help secure new members and make them feel welcome. However, do not neglect loyal older members. They must always feel a part of this club, too. You are also the right hand of the president. Work with her and support her. Be ready to lighten her load whenever possible. Familiarize yourself thoroughly with your club's by-laws and procedures, for you are a president in training. Do you accept this new responsibility? (The officer should answer, "I do.")

(Give the officer a candle to light from the central one. Once it is lit, continue.) In lighting this candle, you have agreed to fulfill your obligations to your club. May you be a welcoming light to this membership.

The president of an organization leads the club. You will preside at all meetings, appoint committees and chairmen, and follow up on club details making sure that things are being done properly and on time. You are also your club's representative to the community. You will be the voice of your club during this term of office. As president, you assume a place of great honor and great obligation. Do you accept this new responsibility? (The officer should answer, "I do."

(Give the officer a candle to light from the central one. Once it is lit, continue.) In lighting this candle, you have agreed to fulfill your obligations to your club. May you be a guiding light to this membership.

The officers of the _____ (name of club) have now been installed and have promised to fulfill their new duties. Keep your club's path well-lit so that members can follow you easily and willingly. Be a light that leads to the successful completion of all club goals and projects. Just as the candles you have lit are now burning brightly, may you, the new officers of this organization, lead your club to a bright future.

Sweet Time

In this ceremony candy bars are used to install the officers. Just as each candy bar on the market has special ingredients that make it distinctive from other bars, the officers of an organization have certain tasks that make their jobs unique. However, there is one element that all of the candy bars in this ceremony share. They all have chocolate in them. Likewise members of an organization share a common thread, a purpose that unites them all in the same goals.

An appropriate gift for each officer would be a candy bar. The following wrapped candies are needed: a Pay Day, a Symphony, a Mounds, a package of plain M & M's, a package of peanut M & M's, a package of Peanut Butter Cups, and a Milky Way. A bag of snack size 3 Musketeers bars will also be needed. These bars are given to the members at the conclusion of the ceremony. Candy bars can be purchased at most stores and are very economical. A quick trip to a store is the only preparation time required.

This ceremony lasts about 10 minutes. It is a lighthearted ceremony that can be used for any group, but would definitely be a hit in a student's organization. Have the script prepared and the candy bars purchased in advance. Before buying the 3 Musketeers bars, find out how many members there are in the organization. You will want to have enough pieces of candy for each member.

INSTALLATION CEREMONY

Chocolate—it's so satisfying, and it's been around for centuries. In North America, the Indians initially used cacao, the bean used in making chocolate, as a food and beverage source as well as a medium of exchange.

During the conquest of Mexico, Spanish soldiers discovered cacao and took it back to Europe. By the mid-17th century serving chocolate in England became a symbol of hospitality, similar to the serving of tea and coffee. Chocolate's popularity greatly increased after vanilla and sugar were added in order to take away the bitter taste.

Eventually chocolate came to the United States, and in 1765 the first chocolate mill was established in North America at Dorchester, Massachusetts. Today, with the countless varieties on the market, chocolate is a booming business.

Tonight, the officers of the _____ (name of club) will be given candy bars as they are installed. Just as each candy bar has different ingredients, each officer in this club has specific duties. Although each candy bar used tonight is unique, they all share one common ingredient—chocolate. Likewise, even though your club officers perform different tasks, they share the same goals. Will the officers please come forward? (Have the officers line up in order with the treasurer first.)

—————————#—————————

The treasurer of this organization will count money, pay bills, collect dues, and give monthly financial statements to this club. At times these various monetary duties might seem to be too much. But do not fear, a tasty kind of money is near. (Pick up candy bar.) May this "Pay Day" help you with your new duties. Let it assist you in meeting all of your club's financial obligations. (Give the candy bar to the officer.)

—————————#—————————

The corresponding secretary of this organization will be the liaison between this club and the public. As you take care of correspondence, remember to represent your group in a fitting manner. Excellent composition requires time and thought. (Pick up candy bar.) May this "Symphony" help you maintain perfect harmony between your club and the community. Let it inspire you to keep all of the lines you write in tune. (Give the candy bar to the officer.)

The secretary of this organization will take numerous notes during each club meeting. These notes are then transformed into accurate minutes and become an essential part of this club's history. Sometimes you may feel overwhelmed by your mountain of notes, sometimes you won't. (Pick up candy bar.) May this "Mounds" help you rewrite your many notes into legible, precise minutes. Let it give you energy to help cut through the paper work. (Give the candy bar to the officer.)

The second vice-president of this organization will be in charge of the program committee. You are also in leadership training and must be ready to perform other duties that might be asked of you by your president. Chairing the program committee, you will find that some programs are plain, while others are real nutty. (Pick up packages of candy.) May these packages of "M & M's," plain and peanut, help you select a variety of programs. Let them assist you in planning successful programs that will interest your entire membership. (Give the packages of candy to the officer.)

The first vice-president of this organization will be in charge of the membership committee. You are also the president's understudy. In this office, you wear two hats—membership and future leader. In the area of membership, you must be able to keep all members interested in club projects, recruit new members, and retain older members. As your club's future leader, it is important to learn about this club's policies and procedures. Your job is like two great flavors combined into one. (Pick up package of candy.) May this package of "Peanut Butter Cups" help you tackle all of your future duties. Let this successful combination lead you to a year of success. (Give the candy bar to the officer.)

The president of this organization is the club's leader. You will preside at all meetings, keep current on club business, follow up on details, and represent this club at all times. You have been given your club's highest honor, and members will follow your leadership. You are now the principal star in this club's galaxy. (Pick up candy bar.) May this "Milky Way" help you lead and shine brightly. Let it show you the way to guide your club to great heights. (Give the candy bar to the officer.

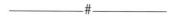

(To the membership.) Club members, you are also an integral part of this organization. Like your officers, you also have special duties and tasks. Your jobs might not be as prominent, but they are as important. Just as all of these candy bars have chocolate in them, all of you, officers and members alike, share the same club goals. Support one another and work together so that this club will become stronger. (Pick up package of candy bars.) A popular trio from France had a famous saying. May their slogan, "One for all and all for one," always be your club's theme. (Give each member a "3 Musketeers" bar.)

Chain Reaction

This ceremony shows how officers and members of a club are united together like a chain. Just as a chain is made up of many links, an organization is comprised of many different types of people. Each link is needed in order for a chain to accomplish its purpose, and each member of a club is essential in order for the group to achieve its goals.

Within the club, the officers are the master links of a chain bringing together the individual segments and bridging the gaps which can exist between members. By successfully carrying out the responsibilities of their offices, they keep the club running efficiently. In a chain, if one link is broken, or missing, it can become ineffective. So, too, if an officer does not perform the duties of his or her office, an organization can become unproductive.

Lengths of chain given as gifts to the incoming officers will emphasize this focus. The chain symbolizes the bond each officer has to one another and to the club. Chains come in a variety of link widths and can be purchased at a hardware store. The pieces should be at least 6 inches long. This gift idea is not expensive, but requires a trip to a store.

This ceremony will last about 10 minutes. It can be used for any organization and is especially appropriate for a men's group. This theme would also lend itself well to the various civic clubs that are linked to larger national organizations. Prepare the script and purchase the pieces of chain prior to the day of the installation. Script preparation includes obtaining the names of the new officers since they are used in the ceremony. Also, before the ceremony, tell the new officers that they will be asked to answer an installation question with the words, "I do."

INSTALLATION CEREMONY

Will the newly elected officers of the _____ (name of club) please come forward? (Have the officers line up in order with the treasurer first.)

A chain is made up of many links. According to Webster's dictionary, a chain is "a flexible series of joined links, usually of metal, used to pull, confine,...or transmit power." This club is like a chain. It is made up of many people who are joined together in a common bond working towards club goals.

Singularly, one link of a chain cannot yield much power. It needs the other links to become strong. Likewise, each member of this club needs the other members to accomplish projects and goals.

Tonight, the officers of this club will be given a piece of chain as they are installed. The chain symbolizes their link to their club and their willingness to be a vital part of the leadership. As officers, they are important links to the club membership.

—————#—————

_____ (name of officer), you have been elected to serve as treasurer. Your duties will include collecting dues, paying bills, and keeping records of all of this club's financial transactions. Your job is the financial link in this organization.

Do you accept these new responsibilities? (Officer should answer, "I do." Give the officer a piece of chain.) Congratulations. You are now installed. Keep your section of the chain strong.

_____ (name of officer), you have been elected to serve as corresponding secretary. Your duties will include writing notes, responding to mail, and making sure that this club has a positive—public image. Your job is the link between the community and this organization.

Do you accept these new responsibilities? (Officer should answer,"I do." Give the officer a piece of chain.) Congratulations. You are now installed. Keep your section of the chain strong.

—————————#—————————

_____ (name of officer), you have been elected to serve as secretary. Your duties will include taking minutes at all meetings and making sure that the records of this club's business are accurate. You are also the keeper of this group's history. Your job links the past and present to the future.

Do you accept these new responsibilities? (Officer should answer, "I do." Give the officer a piece of chain.) Congratulations. You are now installed. Keep your section of the chain strong.

—————————#—————————

_____ (name of officer), you have been elected to serve as second vice-president. Your duties will include serving as the chairman of the program committee and assisting the president when needed. Your job links a variety of programs to a diverse membership.

Do you accept these new responsibilities? (Officer should answer, "I do." Give the officer a piece of chain.) Congratulations. You are now installed. Keep your section of the chain strong.

—————————#—————————

_____ (name of officer), you have been elected to serve as first vice-president. Your duties will include serving as the chairman of the membership committee, supporting and working closely with the president, and learning about all the policies and procedures of this organization. Your job links newer members with seasoned members. Make certain that everyone feels needed and wanted.

Do you accept these new responsibilities? (Officer should answer, "I do." Give the officer a piece of chain.) Congratulations. You are now installed. Keep your section of the chain strong.

—————#—————

_____ (name of officer), you have been elected to serve as president. You have been given the highest honor in your club. Your duties will include presiding at meetings, appointing chairmen and committees, following up on all club matters, and representing your organization at all times. Work with your members and listen to their concerns. Your job is the link between the executive board and the membership.

Do you accept these new responsibilities? (Officer should answer, "I do." Give the officer a piece of chain.) Congratulations. You are now installed. Keep your section of the chain strong.

A chain is only as strong as its weakest link. If one link is broken, or missing, the chain becomes powerless. That is how it is with clubs, too. If one member becomes lost, or one officer fails to fulfill her duties, a link in the club chain is broken.

(To the officers.) Officers, you have agreed to keep the links of your club strong. Serve your members with diligence, integrity, and enthusiasm for you are important links in this organization.

(To the membership.) Members, you are also significant links. Each one of you is an important part of this club and is needed. Give the officers your encouragement, support, and devotion. Like a chain, when members and officers work together, an organization is able to "transmit great power." Keep your club chain strong.

Rainbow

This ceremony uses the colors of the rainbow to install the officers. Just as each color in the spectrum (red, orange, yellow, green, blue, indigo, and violet) has certain characteristics, each officer in a club has definite duties and responsibilities to perform. A beautiful rainbow develops when the seven colors come together. Likewise, an organization runs smoothly when all of the officers perform their jobs proficiently. Each officer is needed to make a club run smoothly, just as each color is essential to make a rainbow.

A single, white, long-stemmed carnation with a long colorful ribbon attached to it is a simple, but elegant gift. Each flower should have a different color of ribbon. Use red, orange, yellow, green, blue, and violet colored ribbon. (Although indigo is briefly mentioned in this ceremony, the color is not used to install an officer.) Near the end of the ceremony, the ribbons are pulled together to form a rainbow. Carnations and ribbon can be purchased at a florist shop. Call in advance to make certain that the florist has the colors of ribbon needed and will have the flowers ready for pickup on the day of the ceremony. If you want to make your own streamers, ribbon can be purchased at a craft store. The ribbon should be one-half inch to 1 inch wide and at least 4 feet long. Preparation time for this gift idea is minimal, especially if the florist decorates the flowers for you. If you decide to decorate the flowers, cut the streamers prior to the day of the ceremony. Time will also be needed on the day of the ceremony to attach the streamers to the flowers. Regardless of which method is used, call the florist to arrange for flower pickup. The cost of this suggestion will vary depending on whether the florist does everything, or not. Overall, it should be fairly inexpensive.

A second gift option would be to give each officer a sun catcher with a long ribbon attached to the top of it. Use colored ribbon one-eighth inch to one-fourth inch wide and at least 4 feet long. Select the same colors as stated in the above paragraph. Sun catchers can be found in gift stores and department stores. If possible, try to find sun catchers that are rainbows. Ribbon can be purchased at a craft store, or at a florist's. This idea demands a greater time commitment and would cost more than the first one.

This ceremony runs between 10 and 15 minutes and can be used by any women's organization. It is also a perfect service for a young women's group. The script should be prepared prior to the ceremony. Make arrangements with the florist to pick up the flowers on the day of the ceremony. If sun catchers are given, have them readied in advance.

INSTALLATION CEREMONY

A rainbow is made up of seven different colors—red, orange, yellow, green, blue, indigo, and violet. Each one of these colors is exquisite. However, when they all come together to form a rainbow, they become unequalled in beauty. Likewise, clubs are made up of many types of people. Each person is unique, but in joining a club, a new member becomes a part of a colorful group unequalled in strength.

Although there are only seven colors in the spectrum, there are over 2 million tints and shades of these basic colors. The tints and shades of the colors can be compared to the many talents and skills that individual members bring to a club. Some members have creative abilities, some have organizational skills, and some have leadership qualities.

Tonight, the officers of the _____ (name of club) will be installed using the colors of the rainbow. Just as each color of the spectrum is distinctive, each office of this club has specific tasks. When officers successfully perform their duties, they help keep their club running smoothly. Will the newly elected officers please come forward? (Have the officers line up with the treasurer first.)

(Give the treasurer her gift.) The color red symbolizes the treasurer. Red represents energy, vitality, and perseverance. It is also known as a sacrificial color, indicating one's willingness to give of oneself.

As treasurer, your duties include collecting all dues and monies, paying all approved bills, and keeping accurate financial records. You will be giving of yourself in many ways to this club as you handle its financial responsibilities. May the red color of your ribbon give you the energy, vitality, and perseverance needed to fulfill these obligations.

(Give the corresponding secretary her gift.) The color orange symbolizes the corresponding secretary. Orange stands for thoughtfulness and consideration.

As corresponding secretary, your duties include handling all of this club's correspondence. Remember to take the time to think before you write. Your words are a reflection of this club and its members. May the orange color of your ribbon always remind you to be thoughtful and considerate.

(Give the secretary her gift.) The color yellow symbolizes the secretary. Considered to be a bright and optimistic color, yellow stands for thought and mental concentration.

As secretary, your duties include keeping an accurate record of all of this club's business. Writing up each meeting's minutes will require a great deal of thought. May the yellow color of your ribbon give you the mental concentration and optimism needed to fulfill your commitment.

(Give the second vice-president her gift.) The color green symbolizes the second vice-president. Green indicates co-operation and peace. A calming, restful color, it also stands for growth and the continuity of life.

As second vice-president, you represent the continuity of leadership. You are second in command to the president and will acquire valuable leadership skills. As chairman of the program committee, you must provide guidance and teach co-operation in the selection of club programs. May the green color of your ribbon keep you calm as you perform the various responsibilities of this office.

(Give the first vice-president her gift.) The color blue symbolizes the first vice-president. Blue represents healing love, faith, loyalty, and inspiration. Like green, blue is another calming color.

As first vice-president, you are in training for the office of president. Your faith and loyalty are important to this club's members, and, especially, to the president who will rely on you for help. As chairman of the membership committee, inspire members, old and new, to become active in your club. As a source of healing love, you must strive to keep members in harmony about projects and goals. May the blue color of your ribbon give you the inspiration needed to face the challenges of this office.

(Give the president her gift.) The color purple symbolizes the president. Purple represents leadership, greatness, and unselfish efforts. A regal color, purple is associated with royalty, or persons of high rank.

As president, you will be treated royally for you have been elected to the highest office in your club. Being president is an honor and a privilege, but with this esteemed office comes many responsibilities. Duties of the office include presiding at all meetings, dealing with internal club matters, and handling any club crises. As president, you are also this club's representative to the community. May the purple color of your ribbon remind you to give unselfishly of yourself as you lead your club.

During this ceremony, each officer has been installed with a different color. Alone, each color is striking, but when the colors come together, a larger, more beautiful thing occurs. (Pull all the streamers together.) A rainbow is created. Each color is needed to make this rainbow, just as each officer is necessary to make this club run properly.

(To the membership.) Members, you are also a part of the rainbow. You are the tints and shades of these basic colors. You bring various talents and skills to this club. Work with your officers, and together you can make this club a beautiful one.

The Best Deal

In this ceremony, a deck of cards is used to illustrate the importance of members and officers within a club. In a deck of cards, every card is necessary. If one card is missing, the deck is considered to be incomplete and useless. In the same manner, every member is essential to the well-being of a club. If one member is missing, there is a hole in the organization. The officers are an integral part of a club's leadership. Specific cards are used to symbolize each officer's particular duties. Like a missing card, if one officer fails to complete her tasks, an organization can become ineffectual.

A deck of cards would be a fitting gift. Six decks are needed, and they can be found at discount department stores, toy stores, and drug stores. Prior to the ceremony, pull out one card from each deck and place it on the outside box with a rubber band. The cards needed are the nine of hearts for the treasurer, the ten of hearts for the corresponding secretary, the jack of hearts for the secretary, the queen of hearts for the second vice-president, the king of hearts for the first vice-president, and the ace of hearts for the president. Preparation requires a quick trip to the store and time to open the decks to pull out the necessary cards. This gift idea should be reasonable in cost.

This ceremony will run between 10 and 15 minutes and is a light ceremony that can be used for any organization. It would be particularly appropriate for a civic organization that hosts annual card parties, or a sports and leisure group. Make certain that the script and gifts are ready prior to the day of the installation. In preparing your script, obtain the new officers' names since they are used in the ceremony.

INSTALLATION CEREMONY

Although the origin of playing cards is unclear, it is believed that the very first cards originated in China or India thousands of years ago. Once cards were introduced into Europe, the Europeans played many different kinds of games with them. Cards became so popular that in the mid-18th century Edmond Hoyle wrote a book describing the rules of almost every known game. Today, cards continue to be a favorite pastime, and people of all ages spend hours playing the various games a deck of cards can provide.

Tonight, the officers of the _____ (name of club) will be installed using a theme of cards. Within a deck, no two cards are alike, and every single card is needed for that deck to be usable. Likewise, within this club, no two officer's duties are the same, and every distinctive task must be completed for this club to have a successful year. Will the newly elected officers please come forward? (Have the officers line up in order with the treasurer first.)

—————#—————

_____ (name of officer), you have been elected to serve as treasurer of this club. Your duties include collecting dues, paying bills, and keeping accurate financial records. (Give the officer the deck of cards with the nine of hearts on top.) The card representing your office is the nine of hearts. In this office, you will find yourself running to the bank quite often. Sometimes it may seem like you are at the bank at least nine times a week. May this nine of hearts remind you of your tasks. Best wishes in your new endeavor.

—————#—————

_____ (name of officer), you have been elected to serve as corresponding secretary of this club. Your duties include taking care of your club's correspondence. (Give the officer the deck of cards with the ten of hearts on top.) The card representing your office is the ten of hearts. Remember to always "take ten" before writing anything because what you say is a reflection upon your club. May this ten of hearts remind you of your tasks. Best wishes in your new endeavor.

———————#———————

_____ (name of officer), you have been elected to serve as secretary of this club. Your duties include taking minutes at all meetings and keeping accurate records of your club's actions. (Give the officer the deck of cards with the jack of hearts on top.) The card representing your office is the jack of hearts. Notice that he is holding a feather. That feather symbolizes the pen that you will be holding as you jot down proceedings that occur at your club's meetings. May this jack of hearts remind you of your tasks. Best wishes in your new endeavor.

———————#———————

_____ (name of officer), you have been elected to serve as second vice-president of this club. Your duties include chairing the program committee and assuming other responsibilities that may be assigned to you by the president. (Give the officer the deck of cards with the queen of hearts on top.) The card representing your office is the queen of hearts. The queen is the third highest card after the ace and king. Likewise, you are your club's third highest leader after the president and first vice-president. Be supportive of your president, and take time to learn valuable leadership qualities. May this queen of hearts remind you of your tasks. Best wishes in your new endeavor.

———————#———————

_____ (name of officer), you have been elected to serve as first vice-president of this club. Your duties include chairing the membership committee and becoming thoroughly familiar with all your club's policies and procedures. (Give the officer the deck of cards with the king of hearts on top.) The card representing your office is the king of hearts. The king is second only to the ace. Likewise, you are now the understudy to the highest office in your club. Work for harmony, keep members interested, and assist your president in every way possible. May this king of hearts remind you of your tasks. Best wishes in your new endeavor.

_____ (name of officer), you have been elected to serve as president of this club. Your duties include presiding at all meetings, appointing committees and chairmen, following up on details, and representing your club at all times. (Give the officer the deck of cards with the ace of hearts on top.) The card representing your office is the ace of hearts. The ace is the highest card. Likewise, you will now assume the highest office in your club. It is an honor and privilege, as well as a great responsibility. Listen to your members and lead with enthusiasm and integrity. May this ace of hearts remind you of your tasks. Best wishes in your new endeavor.

(To the officers.) Officers, note that your cards are all in the suit of hearts. This suit was chosen to symbolize the love, patience, and kindness that you, as leaders, must exhibit to other club members. Alone your cards mean nothing in a game of poker, but when they come together, they are a royal flush, the highest hand. Likewise, alone you can do little, but when you work with one another, you will be able to achieve many club goals.

————————#————————

(To the membership.) Members, you are the rest of the cards in this club's deck. Just as a deck is made up of 52 different cards, this club is made up of many different people who possess various talents and skills. Support your club by using your abilities. And remember, a deck needs every card to be whole. Likewise, your club needs you to be complete.

Give a Hoot

This service likens the distinctive duties of an organization's officers to the characteristics of particular endangered animals. When officers fulfill their various tasks, they contribute to the preservation of their club. Capable leadership is necessary in order for an organization to flourish and grow.

As a memento of the event, give each officer a magnet of their endangered animal. The animals used include an elephant, a beaver, an owl, a parrot, a dolphin, and a bald eagle. Earth and nature stores are a good place to begin in your search for magnets. They can also be found in specialty shops and gift stores. This suggestion requires time to shop and browse, but should be relatively low-priced.

Another gift suggestion is to give each officer a picture of their endangered animal. Go to garage sales, flea markets, rummage sales, and used bookstores to find books, or magazines, that have pictures of the appropriate animals. Once the pictures are found, cut them out, and glue them on to a piece of construction paper. Necessary supplies, other than the pictures, include construction paper, scissors, and rubber cement. Although this idea is economical, it will require a time commitment.

An endangered species poster is a third possibility. Posters of this kind can be found in earth and nature stores. If possible, select posters that have the animals mentioned in the ceremony. This remembrance will probably be more costly than the other two.

This solemn ceremony is about 15 minutes in length and can be used for any group. It would be an ideal service for an environmental organization, or a nature club. The script and gifts should be prepared in advance.

INSTALLATION CEREMONY

Over the years, numerous species of animals have faced the threat of becoming extinct. Causes have included society's carelessness, as well as mother nature's fury. However, since the 1970's, measures have been taken to combat this problem through legislation and education of the populace.

Although the officers in this organization do not face extinction, the decisions they make, while in office, do affect this club's future. If they choose to fulfill their various duties and tasks, a club is preserved and kept off of the endangered list. An organization will thrive and grow under competent leadership.

Tonight, the officers of the _____ (name of club) will be installed using an endangered species theme. Each animal mentioned has unique characteristics that can be compared to the responsibilities of a particular office. Will the newly elected officers please come forward? (Have the officers line up with the treasurer first.)

The animal that represents the treasurer is the Asian elephant. (Give the gift to the officer.) Known as the largest living animal on land, an elephant is a fast learner and has an excellent memory which is utilized in its journeys over extensive areas.

As treasurer, you are in charge of your club's finances and will learn many new skills. Some of your duties include collecting dues, paying bills, and giving a monthly financial report to your club. Like the elephant, may your memory assist you in your journey as treasurer.

———————#———————

The animal that represents the corresponding secretary is the European beaver. (Give the gift to the officer.) A beaver always appears to be working. Instinctively, it builds dams and lodges even if there is no place for another one, and it gathers food to store even if it has more than enough.

As corresponding secretary, you are in charge of your club's correspondence. You will be busy writing, collecting, and storing letters and notes. Like the beaver, may your various tasks become instinctive.

The animal that represents the secretary is the spotted owl. (Give the gift to the officer.) A symbol of wisdom, the owl has very large eyes and sensitive hearing. Over land, it can fly quickly and noiselessly, an attribute that helps in the capture of prey.

As secretary, you are in charge of your club's history. You will need sensitive hearing in order to keep accurate minutes of each meeting. Your minutes tell your club "who" said what and "who" did what. Like the owl, may you exhibit wisdom as your pen flies quickly and noiselessly over paper.

The animal that represents the second vice-president is the Australian parrot. (Give the gift to the officer.) Numbering around 315 different species, parrots are a noisy bird that can become tame and taught to talk. These brightly-colored birds are popular pets.

As second vice-president, you are in charge of the program committee. You will learn that there are as many different kinds of programs as there are species of parrots. Guide your committee so that the programs selected for your club interest the entire membership. Like the parrot, may your programs add color to your club.

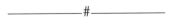

The animal that represents the first vice-president is the Amazon River dolphin. (Give the gift to the officer.) Dolphins have an instinctive sonar system that makes it possible for them to locate objects that are in their path. They also have a keen sense of hearing and excellent vision. Traveling in groups of 100 to 1,000 members, they play and hunt together, as well as protect one another.

As first vice-president, you are in charge of the membership committee. On the well-traveled membership road, play and work with your members. Be attentive to their various needs. As the understudy to your president, help detect any obstacles that might be in your club's path. Like the dolphin, may your eyes and ears always be alert to club members' concerns.

The animal that represents the president is the bald eagle. (Give the gift to the officer.) A symbol of freedom and strength, eagles are considered to be the most powerful birds in the world. Their large wings help them to soar gracefully in the air. Although eagles are courageous birds, they carefully stay away from danger. Eagles are believed to have the keenest sight of all birds, better even than humans.

As president, you are in charge of your club's leadership. You have been given great power, but also have great responsibility. Your duties include presiding at meetings, appointing chairmen and committees, following up on club matters, and providing encouragement. You must show courage, but also be extremely careful to avoid dangers. Like the eagle, use your keen sight to lead this club to new heights where it may soar gracefully under your leadership.

(To the membership.) Members, you also have special attributes that are needed in order for this club to flourish and grow. Support your officers, work with them to achieve goals, and help preserve this organization. Remember, only you can keep this club off of the endangered list.

New Bouquet

Gardens are comprised of numerous species of flowers. Similarly, clubs are made up of various types of people. In this ceremony, different kinds of flowers illustrate the distinctive duties of each club officer. Flowers have certain traits, characteristics, and legends associated with them. Offices of an organization also have specific tasks and duties associated with them. When the members of each office work together, they provide leadership and help a club meet its objectives.

You might give each officer a flowering plant as a keepsake of the occasion. The potted flowers needed are a marigold for the treasurer, a pansy for the corresponding secretary, a daisy for the secretary, a sunflower for the second vice-president, a zinnia for the first vice-president, and a rose bush for the president. Flowers can be purchased at a greenhouse, a florist's, or a discount department store. For decoration, have colored foil placed around the pots. Depending on the time of the year, or the garden zone in which you live, these plants might not be available, and you will have to use one of the other gift suggestions. This idea should be relatively low priced. Preparation time includes a trip to the store to buy the plants.

An alternative is to give each officer, except for the president, a package of seeds. The seeds needed are marigolds for the treasurer, pansies for the corresponding secretary, daisies for the secretary, sunflowers for the second vice-president, and zinnias for the first vice-president. A small rose bush is needed for the president. Seeds can be purchased at a discount department store, or ordered through a seed catalog. The rose bush can be found at a greenhouse, or a discount department store. Seed catalogs often have rose bushes, too. If you buy the seeds and rose bush through a catalog, make sure that you order them weeks prior to the ceremony so that they arrive in plenty of time. Once again, time of the year and the garden zone in which you live might dictate whether or not this gift idea can be used. This proposal has the advantage of being reasonable in cost. Preparation time varies depending on whether the items are ordered, or purchased in your vicinity.

A set of note cards with the appropriate flower on them is a third option. These will probably have to be made although you might be able to find them ready-made at a craft store. Purchase six sets of plain note cards. Buy stencils, or make stencils, of the flowers needed. Stencils can be made out of heavy cardboard. Find a picture of the correct flower, trace it onto the cardboard, then cut out the cardboard between the lines, making certain that you leave the center lines intact as part of the stencil. The flowers required include a marigold, a pansy, a daisy, a sunflower, a zinnia, and a rose. With a stencil brush and paints, stencil the fronts of each set of note cards with the flower that corresponds to that particular office. Supplies needed include pictures of the necessary flowers, scissors, cardboard, tracing paper, stencil paints, a stencil brush, and note cards. This idea demands a time commitment, but should not be expensive.

This ceremony is about 15 minutes in length. A solemn ceremony, it can be used for any women's group, but is best suited for a garden or nature club. The script and gifts should be prepared in advance. The script will need to be changed if the third gift idea is used. The words, "symbol of a," found in parentheses in the ceremony, are to be read since an actual flower is not being given to each officer as a gift.

INSTALLATION CEREMONY

There are at least 250,000 known species of flowering plants. Over the centuries, they have been cultivated for beauty, grown for food, raised for medicinal and cosmetic purposes, and utilized for house-hold means. Flowers have also been associated with many legends and beliefs throughout the ages.

Tonight, the officers of the _____ (name of club) will be installed using a theme of flowers. Just as each flower has certain characteristics and folklore associated with it, each officer of this club has specific duties and tasks associated with the office. Will the newly elected officers please come forward? (Have officers line up in order with the treasurer first.)

———————#———————

The marigold is the flower that symbolizes the treasurer. Marigold means "Mary's gold" and is considered to be a powerful good luck charm. Your duties will include collecting and depositing money, writing checks, and giving a monthly financial statement to your club. (Pick up the gift.) As you handle your "club's gold," may this (symbol of a) marigold bring you good luck. Best wishes for a thriving year. (Give the gift to the officer.)

———————#———————

The pansy is the flower that symbolizes the corresponding secretary. Coming from the French word pensee, pansy means "thought" and is often associated with thinking good thoughts about one's loved one. Your duties will include writing letters and taking care of your club's correspondence. (Pick up the gift.) As you write your letters, may this (symbol of a) pansy provide you with good thoughts. Best wishes for a thriving year. (Give the gift to the officer.)

———————#———————

The daisy is the flower that symbolizes the secretary. Daisies were believed to have fortune-telling powers, especially in the area of love. Many young maidens picked off the petals while chanting, "He loves me. He loves me not." Your duties will include taking minutes at all club meetings and preserving the historical records of your club. (Pick up the gift.) As you write up your club's various actions, may this (symbol of a) daisy help you correctly record, "The club passed this. The club passed this not." Best wishes for a thriving year. (Give the gift to the officer.)

———————#———————

The sunflower is the flower that symbolizes the second vice-president. Considered to be a representation of the sun, this flower has been used for a variety of purposes. The Indians worshiped it, used it to dress their hair, and cooked with it. The American pioneers harvested the seeds for food, the stalks for cloth, and the blossoms for dye. Your duties will include chairing the program committee and assisting your president. (Pick up the gift.) As you guide the program committee, may this (symbol of a) sunflower remind you of the diversity of your membership and help your committee select a variety of programs for the upcoming year. Best wishes for a thriving year. (Give the gift to the officer.)

———————#———————

The zinnia is the flower that symbolizes the first vice-president. Originally found in the wilds of Mexico, zinnias have been called "youth and old age." It received this nickname because its old flowers continued to flourish and stay fresh even while its new ones bloomed. Your duties will include chairing the membership committee and working closely with your president. (Pick up the gift.) As you work with the membership committee, may this (symbol of a) zinnia help you keep new and old members, "youth and old age," excited about this club and its projects. Best wishes for a thriving year. (Give the gift to the officer.)

———————#———————

The rose is the flower that symbolizes the president. Unparalleled in beauty to any other flower, the rose is considered to be the "queen flower." It is cultivated for its beauty, medicinal uses, and distinctive fragrance. Grace and elegance are associated with the rose. Your duties will include presiding at all club meetings, appointing committees and chairmen, keeping up on all club matters, and representing your club. You now hold your club's highest office which makes you the "queen" member of your organization. (Pick up the gift.) As you lead your club, may this (symbol of a) rose help you fulfill your many new duties with grace and elegance. Best wishes for a thriving year. (Give the gift to officer.)

(To the membership.) Members, you are the other flowers in this club's garden. Your attributes are important and needed in order for this club to achieve its goals. When you support one another and work together, your club will flourish and grow. Best wishes for a thriving year.

Fruitful Future

Fruit is an important part of any diet. It contains many necessary vitamins and minerals which help to keep a body healthy. In the same manner, officers are essential to an organization. They perform many distinctive duties and tasks that help to keep their club running smoothly. Many types of fruit are combined to make a fruit basket; so too, various kinds of people join together to form a club. As leaders, the officers must learn to cooperate and encourage cooperation among the membership so that everyone is united in goals.

A gift suggestion for each officer would be a fruit basket that contains all of the fruits mentioned in the ceremony. The fruits used are an apricot for the treasurer, a peach for the corresponding secretary, a pineapple for the secretary, a lemon for the second vice-president, a bunch of grapes for the first vice-president, and an apple for the president. Since six baskets are to be made, one for each officer, buy six of each of the above fruits. Fresh fruit is preferred, but if it is unavailable, or off-season, canned or dried fruit can be used. Fruit can be bought at a grocery store, or a farmer's market. Discount department stores and craft stores carry baskets. The baskets should be large enough to hold six items of fruit, but not so large that they look empty when the fruit is placed inside. Preparation time includes going to the store to find and buy the baskets and fruit. Once all of the items are purchased, additional time is needed to assemble the baskets. Cost will vary depending on the price of the selected baskets and the season of the year. Baskets can be expensive, and certain fruit items do cost more during their off-season.

This ceremony runs between 10 and 15 minutes. It is a solemn ceremony that can be used for any organization, but would be well-suited for a garden or nature club. Have the script and gifts ready prior to the day of the installation. Preparation of the script includes obtaining the new officers' names since they are to be used in the ceremony.

INSTALLATION CEREMONY

Fruit contains many needed vitamins and minerals and is an important part of a well-balanced diet. Labeled "Nature's Medicine," fruit helps to keep a body healthy. The adage, "an apple a day keeps the doctor away," is considered to be quite accurate. An integral part of leadership, the officers of a club help to keep it healthy. Their jobs include many tasks and duties that must be realized in order for their organization to accomplish its goals.

Tonight, the officers of the _____ (name of club) will be installed using a theme of fruit. Fruit baskets symbolize how officers work together. Just as each piece of fruit has different vitamins and minerals, each officer has distinctive duties to perform. A fruit basket is a combination of various kinds of fruit. Likewise, a successful club is the end result of each officer's cooperation. Will the newly elected officers please come forward? (Have the officers line up in order with the treasurer first.)

——————#——————

_____ (name of treasurer), you have been elected to serve as treasurer. The fruit that symbolizes your office is the apricot. An apricot is high in iron content and rich in minerals. It is useful in cases of anemia, bronchitis, and asthma.

As treasurer, you are in charge of the riches of your club. Your duties include collecting and depositing money, writing checks, and giving a monthly financial statement to your club. Like the apricot, the fulfillment of your duties will help keep your club's finances anemic-free. (Give the officer a fruit basket.) Congratulations.

————————#————————

_____ (name of corresponding secretary), you have been elected to serve as corresponding secretary. The fruit that symbolizes your office is the peach. A peach can improve the health of the skin and give color to the complexion.

As corresponding secretary, you are in charge of your club's appearance. Your duties include writing letters and notes that cultivate a positive image of your club. Like the peach, the fulfillment of your duties will help keep your club's healthy "peaches and cream" complexion. (Give the officer a fruit basket.) Congratulations.

————————#————————

_____ (name of secretary), you have been elected to serve as secretary. The fruit that symbolizes your office is the pineapple.A pineapple contains the enzyme papain and the element chlorine. Papain and chlorine aid in digestion.

As secretary, you are in charge of absorbing the actions of your club. Your duties include taking minutes at every meeting and keeping your club's historical records. Like the pineapple, the fulfillment of your duties will help keep your club's decisions digested and preserved for the future. (Give the officer a fruit basket.) Congratulations.

————————#————————

_____ (name of second vice-president), you have been elected to serve as second vice-president. The fruit that symbolizes your office is the lemon. A lemon is loaded with vitamin C and has various uses. It can be an antiseptic for cuts; eliminate stains from teeth; treat dandruff; lessen the itch of an insect bite; aid with a cold, fever, or headache; comfort a sore throat; and even be used for wrinkles.

As second vice-president, you are in charge of providing variety for your club. Your duties include chairing the program committee and assisting the president when needed. As program chairman, guide your committee so that various kinds of programs are selected. Like the lemon, the fulfillment of your duties will help keep your club's diverse membership interested. (Give the officer a fruit basket.) Congratulations.

————————#————————

_____ (name of first vice-president), you have been elected to serve as first vice-president. The fruit that symbolizes your office is the grape. Known as one of the world's oldest cultivated fruits, the grape is a blood and body builder and a quick source of energy.

As first vice-president, you are in charge of building up your club. Your duties include chairing the membership committee, keeping all members, old and new, excited and informed about club functions, and working closely with the president. Like the grape, the fulfillment of your duties will help keep your club energized. (Give the officer a fruit basket.) Congratulations.

————————#————————

_____ (name of president), you have been elected to serve as president. The fruit that symbolizes your office is the apple. An apple contains important minerals and vitamins that help strengthen the blood. Eaten daily, an apple can prevent emotional upsets, tension, and headaches.

As president, you are in charge of strengthening your club and averting tension. Your duties include presiding at meetings, appointing committees and chairmen, encouraging members, and representing your club at all times. You hold the highest office your club can give and have the greatest responsibility. Like the apple, the fulfillment of your duties will help keep your club free from emotional upsets and headaches. (Give the officer a fruit basket.) Congratulations.

(To the membership.) Members, you are also a part of this fruit basket. Just as each piece of fruit is necessary to a proper diet, every club member is vital to this organization. Your talents, skills, and abilities are needed in order for this club to be complete. Like a fruit basket, work with one another to make your club healthy, successful, and well-balanced.

Laugh Time

Gag gifts provide humor in the following installation service. As the officers are installed, they are given symbolic gifts that represent the distinctive duties of their particular positions. The gifts given serve to remind the executives that the fulfillment of their specific tasks is important to their club. When officers successfully perform their duties, they help their club achieve its goals.

Give each officer a humorous gag gift. The appropriate items needed include play money for the treasurer; a rubber pencil for the corresponding secretary; an eraser for the secretary; a joke book for the second vice-president; a solid-colored baseball cap, that has two small signs attached to it, for the first vice-president; and a large bottle of aspirin for the president. Small bottles of glue are also needed for the membership. This idea requires time to find and purchase the necessary items. In addition, two small signs for the first vice-president's hat must be made in advance. Use two small index cards and a black marker. Write the words "membership" on one card and the words "presidential understudy" on the other. Attach the cards to the opposite sides of the hat with scotch tape, or masking tape. Many of the items required for this ceremony can be found in discount department stores, drug stores, toy stores, or specialty shops that carry gag items. This suggestion should be fairly inexpensive.

Light-hearted and brief, this ceremony lasts about 10 minutes and can be used for any organization, especially a men's group. Preparation includes having the script ready and the gifts purchased prior to the day of the installation. Since each member receives a small container of glue at the conclusion of the ceremony, make sure you get the correct number of members attending ahead of time.

INSTALLATION CEREMONY

Officers of a club have distinctive duties. One signs checks, another writes letters, and another presides at meetings. In order for a club to run smoothly and be effective, the officers must carry out their respective duties.

Tonight, the officers of the _____ (name of club) will be installed with symbolic gifts that represent each particular office and its tasks. Although the gifts are humorous, the responsibilities of each office are not. Club goals can only be accomplished when officers successfully fulfill their obligations. Will the newly elected officers please come forward? (Have the officers line up in order with the treasurer first.)

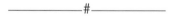

The duties of the treasurer include collecting dues, depositing money, and giving the club a monthly financial statement. To assist you in your new endeavors is this gift of play money. May it remind you that club funds are nothing to play around with. (Give the gift to the officer.)

———————#———————

The duties of the corresponding secretary include writing notes and letters. To assist you in your new endeavors is this gift of a rubber pencil. May it remind you that correspondence is not a laughing matter, but is something that must be dealt with quickly and efficiently. (Give the gift to the officer.)

The duties of the secretary include taking minutes at club meetings and keeping your club's historical records. To assist you in your new endeavors is this gift of an eraser. May it remind you that accuracy in recording your club's actions is extremely important. (Give the gift to the officer.)

The duties of the second vice-president include chairing the program chairman and assisting the president. Keeping in mind your diverse membership, help your committee select a wide range of interesting programs. To assist you in your new endeavors is this gift of a joke book. May it remind you that a variety of programs keeps everybody happy. (Give the gift to the officer.)

The duties of the first vice-president include chairing the membership committee and working closely with the president. It is essential that all members, old and new, become involved in club projects. You must also take time to learn about your organization's many policies and procedures. To assist you in your new endeavors is this gift of a two-sided baseball cap. May it remind you that you have two jobs—membership chairman and presidential understudy. Both are vital to the welfare of your club. (Give the gift to the officer.)

The duties of the president include presiding at all meetings, appointing committees and chairmen, and encouraging club members. You have been given a great honor that holds great responsibility. You are the person to whom your club looks for guidance. To assist you in your new endeavors is this gift of a bottle of aspirin. May it remind you that effective and efficient leadership alleviates club headaches. (Give the gift to the officer.)

(To the membership.) Members, you are the final components in this club. Like the officers, you also have significant duties to perform. Your tasks include supporting your officers, working at club functions, and giving of your time and talents to benefit your organization. To assist you in your endeavors is this gift of a bottle of glue. May it remind you that you are the glue that holds your organization together. Without you, there would not be a club. Work together, and you can achieve great things. (Give out gifts to the membership.)

Sparkle Plenty

In this ceremony, gems are used to represent the distinctive duties of each officer. Individual gems have definite traits and characteristics. Likewise, each officer in a club has specific duties and tasks. Gems are cherished for their great value. In the same manner, officers are prized for their dedication and willingness to serve.

A pin that has the officer's symbolic gem in it would make a nice keepsake of the event. The gems used in the ceremony are an emerald, an opal, an amethyst, a sapphire, a ruby, and a diamond. This idea requires going to a jewelry store to find, or to order, six pins. It is not necessary that all of the pins be identical. Purchase pins that lend themselves to having a gem placed on them, then ask a jeweler to place the correct gem fragments on the pins. Gem fragments are generally low priced, but it is wise to check on the cost in advance. Sometimes the jeweler will even give you the fragments at no charge. If this gift suggestion is used, see a jeweler weeks in advance of the ceremony. Give yourself plenty of time for the pins to be made, or to be ordered. Cost for this idea would vary depending on the pins selected; however, it could be quite expensive. Although your preparation time is minimal, the jeweler needs time. Do not wait until the last moment.

You might give each officer a bookmark that has her symbolic gem in it. The gems needed include an emerald, an opal, an amethyst, a sapphire, a ruby, and a diamond. Purchase bookmarks that are made of heavier paper and have a center top hole with a cord. They can be found at bookstores, gift shops, or discount department stores. Select bookmarks that have an inspirational quote, or saying, on them. It is not necessary that the six bookmarks be identical. Remove the cords from the top of the bookmarks, then take them to a jeweler and ask him to put a gem fragment in the top center hole of each bookmark. Make arrangements with a jeweler in advance, and give him enough time to place the fragments on the bookmarks. A list of the gems needed should also be given to him. The cost for this idea depends on the price of the gem fragments. Bookmarks are generally inexpensive. Preparation time includes purchasing the bookmarks, removing the cords, and going to the jeweler's. Remember that the jeweler needs time, so plan ahead.

This ceremony runs between 10 and 15 minutes. It is a solemn ceremony that is appropriate for any women's organization, or young women's group. Have the script and gifts ready prior to the day of the ceremony. Preparation of the script should include obtaining the names of the new officers since they are used in the ceremony.

INSTALLATION CEREMONY

Since prehistoric days, man has been fascinated by and drawn to rare and precious stones. At one time, gems were believed to have supernatural characteristics and qualities. They were used to guard against evil spirits, generate cures for illnesses, and bring the bearer good luck. Today gems are used for decoration and adornment.

Each individual gem has characteristics that are unique to it. Some are known for their brilliance, some for their hardness, and others for their ability to refract light. Likewise officers of a club have duties that are distinctive to a particular office. One will take minutes, one will write letters, and another will preside at meetings.

Once a gem is cut, polished, and appropriately placed in a setting, it is transformed and becomes a jewel. So too, once officers are installed and placed into their appropriate offices, they are transformed and become a vital part of an organization. Just as a jewel is cherished by its owner, the officers become the jewels of the club and are treasured by the membership. Will the newly elected officers of the _____ (name of club) please come forward? (Have officers line up in order with the treasurer first.)

———————#———————

The treasurer's symbolic gem is an emerald. Believed to bring riches to its wearer, the word emerald comes from the Greek and means "green stone." At one time, all green stones were probably considered to be emeralds.

_____ (name of officer), your duties include collecting and depositing money, writing checks, and keeping records of all of your club's financial transactions. May the green of the emerald remind you of the riches that your club has entrusted to your care. (Give the officer the gift.)

———————#———————

The corresponding secretary's symbolic gem is an opal. One unique characteristic of this stone is its iridescence. Opals have the ability to reflect light in a rainbow-like play of colors that changes with the movement of the gem, or the angle of observation.

_____ (name of officer), your duties include taking care of your club's correspondence and projecting a positive club image to the community. May the iridescence of the opal remind you of the glow your writings must have. (Give the officer the gift.)

———————#———————

The secretary's symbolic gem is an amethyst. This gem is generally purple or violet in color. It was thought to bring good luck and ensure constancy to its owner.

_____ (name of officer), your duties include taking minutes at all club meetings and preserving the historical records of your club. Make certain that your minutes are accurate accounts of your club's many actions. May this amethyst bring you good luck in your new office, and may your minutes ensure constancy within your club. (Give the officer the gift.)

The second vice-president's symbolic gem is a sapphire. The sapphire is usually light blue in color with just a hint of violet. However, it can also be found in the colors of yellow, orange, green, pink, and brown.

_____ (name of officer), your duties include chairing the program committee and learning important leadership skills as you serve under your president. Like the sapphire, that can be found in various colors, may your programs for the coming year be a pleasing and colorful variety for the membership. May this sapphire remind you of the diversity of your membership as you strive to meet their numerous interests. (Give the officer the gift.)

The first vice-president's symbolic gem is a ruby. It was so named because of its red color. One of the most expensive gems, the ruby is the hardest mineral to be found after the diamond.

_____ (name of officer), your duties include chairing the membership committee and working closely with your president. You are the president's understudy and her right hand. Be ready to assist her at any given time. Also, work closely with the membership. Keep all members interested and excited about club projects. May this ruby remind you that you now hold the highest office in your club after your president. (Give the officer the gift.)

The president's symbolic gem is the diamond. The most highly valued of all gem stones, the word diamond comes from the Greek and means "unconquerable." Nothing else compares to its hardness, making it nearly imperishable. A beautiful gem that has many facets, the diamond has been used for adornment since early times.

_____ (name of officer), your duties include presiding at all club meetings, appointing committees and chairmen, following up on club matters, and representing your club. You have been elected to your club's highest office and have been entrusted with the leadership and direction of your club.

May this diamond remind you of your many tasks. You are a beautiful gem that is highly esteemed by your club, and like a diamond, your position, as president, has many facets. Be strong, as the diamond is, and you will be able to meet all the challenges this office holds. (Give the officer the gift.)

(To the membership.) Your officers have now been installed; however, they are not the only gems in this organization. Members, you are the other jewels that make this club complete. You bring various talents, skills, and abilities to this group. Just as an individual gem has unique characteristics, each one of you has special qualities. Support one another and, together, you will have a brilliant year that sparkles and shines as you achieve club goals.

A Pinch Will Do You

In this ceremony, different kinds of herbs are used to represent the officers and their duties. Over the years, certain characteristics and legends have been associated with herbs. Likewise, definite tasks and responsibilities are linked to particular offices. Herbs give recipes added flavor and zest. Officers add flavor and zest to a club by providing valuable leadership and helping members achieve goals.

One gift suggestion would be to give each officer a potted herb. The herbs needed are dill for the treasurer, basil for the corresponding secretary, marjoram for the secretary, chamomile for the second vice-president, lavender for the first vice-president, and sage for the president. Potted herbs, which grow in most areas, can be purchased at a greenhouse, or sometimes found at discount department stores. However, if you live in an area where these herbs are unavailable, use one of the other gift ideas. Season of the year might also preclude this gift option. Cost should be moderate since herbs are fairly inexpensive. Preparation is minimal, but it will take time to visit a greenhouse and purchase the herbs.

Another possibility is to give each officer a dried herb. A container of dill, basil, marjoram, and sage can be given to the treasurer, corresponding secretary, secretary, and president respectively. A box of chamomile tea can be given to the second vice-president, and a lavender sachet can be given to the first vice-president. The containers of herbs can be purchased in the spice section of a grocery store or at a discount department store. The box of tea can also be found at a grocery store. Look for a lavender sachet in a gift store, or discount department store. This gift idea would require more time to locate and purchase the necessary items; however, it should be reasonable in cost.

Herb plant markers could also be given as a remembrance of the occasion. Markers can be found in mail order catalogs, gift shops, and garden centers. If possible, try to find markers that already have the herbs' names on them. The six herbs used in the ceremony are stated in the former gift ideas. Copper plant markers with the appropriate herb name engraved on them could also be given. Engraving can be done with a blunt instrument. Preparation includes locating and purchasing the markers. If engraving is to be done, allow additional time. This option would probably be moderate.

The following ceremony is between 10 and 15 minutes in length. It is a solemn ceremony that can be used for any organization, but would be best suited for a garden or nature club. The script and gifts should be prepared in advance.

INSTALLATION CEREMONY

Herbs are used for a variety of purposes just as clubs are comprised of many different kinds of people. They have been grown for ceremony and magic, medicine, decoration, household uses, beauty aids, and culinary purposes. In cooking, herbs give food added flavor and zest. Likewise, in an organization, officers give a club leadership and guidance.

Tonight, the officers of the _____ (name of club) will be installed using a theme of herbs. Just as individual herbs have specific characteristics and beliefs associated with them, each officer of this club has certain tasks and duties associated with their office. Will the newly elected officers please come forward? (Have the officers line up in order with the treasurer first.)

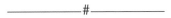

The herb chosen for the newly elected treasurer is dill. (Give the gift to the officer.) In biblical times, dill was considered to be of great value and could be used to pay taxes. It has also been known to soothe digestion and cure hiccups.

As treasurer, your duties include collecting all dues and monies, making deposits, and keeping accurate financial records. Dill represents your great value to this club. May it help you fulfill your duties and soothe the financial worries from your fellow club members' brows. Congratulations and best wishes.

The herb chosen for the newly elected corresponding secretary is basil. (Give the gift to the officer.) Known as a symbol of love, basil was placed on young women's window sills to let prospective suitors know that they were welcome.

As corresponding secretary, your duties include taking care of all of your club's correspondence and promoting your club within the community. Basil represents your eagerness to welcome prospective members into your organization. May it help you fulfill your duties and show love to others. Congratulations and best wishes.

The herb chosen for the newly elected secretary is marjoram. (Give the gift to the officer.) A symbol of happiness, marjoram was often given in, or on, a wedding present because it was believed that it would guarantee a happy marriage. Its leaves make a fragrant polish and can be rubbed on furniture and floors.

As secretary, your duties include taking minutes at all club meetings. Marjoram represents your desire to add polish to your organization by keeping accurate records. May it help you fulfill your duties and guarantee happiness within your club. Congratulations and best wishes.

The herb chosen for the newly elected second vice-president is chamomile. (Give the gift to the officer.) Chamomile has been known to settle indigestion, encourage sleep, and provide relaxation. A chamomile facial steam will brighten up dull, tired skin.

As second vice-president, your duties include chairing the program committee. Chamomile represents your dedication to find programs that will brighten up your organization. May it help you fulfill your duties and provide a relaxed club environment. Congratulations and best wishes.

The herb chosen for the newly elected first vice-president is lavender. (Give the gift to the officer.) Known for its unique fragrance, lavender is used to make sachets. It can also calm nerves, prevent headaches, and induce pleasant dreams.

As first vice-president, your duties include chairing the membership committee and working closely with your president. Lavender represents your willingness to keep all members, old and new, informed about club projects and functions. May it help you fulfill your duties and induce pleasantness and prevent headaches among your club's membership. Congratulations and best wishes.

The herb chosen for the newly elected president is sage. (Give the gift to the officer.) Sage is a highly valued herb. At one time, the Chinese traded the Dutch three chests of tea for one chest of sage. It is also a powerful healing herb.

As president, your duties include presiding at every meeting, appointing committees and chairmen, and making sure that club matters are handled properly. Your club has elected you to its highest position. It brings great responsibility, as well as great honor. Sage represents your willingness to assume the duties of president, an office in which you will be highly valued by your membership. May it help you fulfill your duties and heal any differences that may arise. Congratulations and best wishes.

The new officers have now been installed. However, they are not the only herbs in this garden. (To the membership.) Members, you are the other herbs. Just as an herb has certain lore and characteristics associated with it, each member brings special qualities and traits to this club. You are important and needed in order for this club to accomplish its goals. Support your new officers, work with them, and, together, your club will be beautiful, useful, and full of zest.

Hallelujah

Hymn books contain many different kinds of hymns. Topics range from worship to guidance, from Christmas to Easter, and everything in between. Various types of hymns are put together in a song book that can be used by Christians year round. Clubs are similar to hymn books. They are comprised of various kinds of people who are united in the same goals. Members' diverse talents and skills blend together to make an effective club. Within an organization, the officers are an integral part of its leadership. They guide and direct the membership just as hymns provide guidance and direction for a Christian.

As a memento of the event, give each officer the sheet music of their song. The songs used in the ceremony are "We Give Thee But Thine Own" for the treasurer, "I Will Sing the Wondrous Story" for the corresponding secretary, "I Love To Tell the Story" for the secretary, "In Christ There Is No East or West" for the second vice-president, "Blest Be the Tie That Binds" for the first vice-president, and "All The Way My Savior Leads Me" for the president. Sheet music might need to be ordered, so go to a Christian bookstore several weeks, or months, in advance of the ceremony. This could be a high priced gift.

You might give each officer a copy of their song. The songs can be torn out of old hymn books, or copied. Since all of the hymns used in this ceremony are in the public domain, copies can be made without copyright infringement. The hymns, or copies, should be glued onto construction paper. Supplies needed include old hymn books, or copies of hymns; scissors; construction paper; and rubber cement.

You could also have the hymn scanned at a full service copy center and printed on the paper of your choice. Old hymn books can be found at flea markets, garage sales, rummage sales, thrift stores, second-hand bookstores, and churches. Construction paper and rubber cement can be purchased at a discount department store, or a craft store. This idea is economical, but does require time to find the songs in old hymn books, copy the songs, and glue the hymns onto the paper, or have the songs computer scanned and printed.

Another alternative is to give each officer a rolled up copy of their hymn. Ribbon can be used to tie the roll together. Once again, the songs can be found in old hymn books, copied, or printed by a personal computer. In addition to the hymns, ribbon is also needed. A musical ribbon would be appropriate, but, if unavailable, any color or design can be used. Ribbon can be purchased at craft stores, fabric stores, and discount department stores. This idea requires time to locate the songs, purchase ribbon, roll up the songs, and tie ribbon around them; however, it has the advantage of being reasonable in cost.

This ceremony is about 20 minutes in length. A solemn service, it can be used for any organization, but is best suited for a religious group, or a musical society. It is important to have the script and gifts ready before the day of the installation. The service requires that the first verse of each hymn be sung. Obtaining a pianist and vocalist are part of the pre-ceremony preparations. If you cannot find a vocalist, the members of the organization could sing the first verse of each song. However, a pianist is still necessary and copies of each hymn should be distributed to the membership before the service begins. Also, as you put the script together, find out the names of the new officers that are to be installed.

INSTALLATION CEREMONY

Since the beginnings of Christianity, Christians have loved to sing. Early chants and psalms evolved to original lyrics and tunes, and music has become an important part of worship. Hymn topics vary according to the season of the year and the subject of the day's sermon. Thanksgiving, guidance, adoration, encouragement, and love are just a few of the themes used in the songs that come together to make up a hymn book.

Officers of a club can be compared to a hymn book. They are an important part of a club's leadership and have distinctive duties. One might collect money, another might chair the membership committee, and another might preside at meetings. In order for a club to be efficient, all of the officers must successfully fulfill their required tasks.

Tonight, the officers of the _____ (name of club) will be installed using hymns. Each hymn's theme is different, and it represents the duties of a certain office. Officers guide a club just as hymns provide guidance for a Christian. Will the newly elected officers please come forward? (Have the officers line up with the treasurer first.)

(The first verse of "We Give Thee But Thine Own" should be sung.) _____ (name of officer), you have been elected to serve as treasurer. In this office, you will be in charge of the finances of this club. Your office is not only a trust from your fellow club members, but it is also a trust from God. Remember, the words of your song, "All that we have is Thine alone, A trust, O Lord, from Thee." May God grant you wisdom as you serve your club. (Give the gift to the officer.)

(The first verse of "I Will Sing the Wondrous Story" should be sung.) _____ (name of officer), you have been elected to serve as corresponding secretary. In this office, you will be in charge of all of this club's correspondence. Your job is not only to sing of God's love for us, but you must also sing the wondrous story of your club. It may be the only story your community hears. Remember the words of your song, "Yes, I'll sing the wondrous story of the Christ who died for me,

Sing it with the saints in glory gathered by the crystal sea." May God grant you wisdom as you serve your club. (Give the gift to the officer.)

———————#———————

(The first verse of "I Love To Tell the Story" should be sung.) _____ (name of officer), you have been elected to serve as secretary. In this office, you will be in charge of keeping accurate minutes of every meeting. Your records must be honest and true, just as God's story is true to us. Remember the words of your song, "I love to tell the story, Because I know 'tis true." May God grant you wisdom as you serve your club. (Give the gift to the officer.)

———————#———————

(The first verse of "In Christ There Is No East or West" should be sung.) _____ (name of officer), you have been elected to serve as second vice-president. In this office, you will be the chairman of the program committee. Your job is to find a varied selection of programs that interest a diverse membership. Although God has made all of your members different, they are united within this club. Remember the words of your song, "But one great fellowship of love throughout the whole wide earth." May God grant you wisdom as you serve your club. (Give the gift to the officer.)

———————#———————

(The first verse of "Blest Be the Tie That Binds" should be sung.) _____ (name of officer), you have been elected to serve as first vice-president. In this office, you will be the chairman of the membership committee. Your job is a two-fold position. You must support your president, as well as keep members interested in your club's projects. Remember the words of your song, "Blest be the tie that binds...The fellowship of kindred minds." May God grant you wisdom as you serve your club. (Give the gift to the officer.)

———————#———————

(The first verse of "All the Way My Savior Leads Me" should be sung.) _____ (name of officer), you have been elected to serve as president. In this office, you will be responsible for the leadership and direction of this club. You have been given your club's highest honor, as well as its greatest responsibility. Seek God's help, and He will give you grace and support during your term of office. Remember the words of your song, "All the way my Savior leads me. What have I to ask beside? Can I doubt His tender mercy, Who through life has been my guide?" May God grant you wisdom as you serve your club. (Give the gift to the officer.)

——————#——————

(The first verse of "The Church's One Foundation" should be sung. To the membership.) Members, you are the other themes in this hymn book. Although your jobs are different from the officers', you share the same goals and purposes. Above all, you are united to Jesus Christ. Live a life that is pleasing to God in all that you say and do. Remember the words of your song, "From heaven He came and sought her to be His holy bride; With His own blood He bought her, And for her life He died." May God grant all of you wisdom as you serve your club.

Puzzle Pieces

In this ceremony, the pieces of a jigsaw puzzle symbolize the members of an organization. Every piece of a puzzle is needed to make it complete, and every member of a club is essential to make it whole. The officers of an organization provide support and guidance to the members. Working together, they are the leadership pieces that keep club members united in common goals.

A fitting gift for each officer is a piece of a jigsaw puzzle. Buy a large puzzle and put it together. On the day of the ceremony, transport the puzzle to where the installation is to be held, and place it on a table. Because the puzzle might need some minor repairs after the trip, plan to arrive at your destination early. The six pieces required for the service should be removed and placed on the table near the puzzle. During the ceremony, the officers are asked to complete the puzzle with their pieces. The finished puzzle should then be given to the president. Five smaller puzzles can be purchased as remembrances for the other officers. The smaller puzzles and the empty box of the larger puzzle are to be given to the officers and the president at the same time they receive their puzzle pieces during the ceremony. Puzzles can be found at discount department stores, toy stores, and sometimes card and gift stores. This is a moderately priced idea. Preparation includes the trip to the store to buy the puzzles, and the time needed to put together the president's jigsaw puzzle. Do not wait until the last minute since large puzzles often require many hours.

This ceremony should last between 10 and 15 minutes. A light ceremony that can be used for any organization, this theme is well suited for an educational association since these groups help students put ideas and thoughts together. It would also be appropriate for a sports and leisure club. Make certain that the script is ready prior to the day of the installation. Preparation includes informing the new officers, before the ceremony, that they will be required to answer an installation question with the words, "I do." Buy the puzzles in advance, and allot time to put one together.

INSTALLATION CEREMONY

Puzzles are a part of our daily lives. There are crossword puzzles, number puzzles, and jigsaw puzzles. Children learn to work puzzles at an early age, and this process of figuring out how everything fits together continues throughout adulthood.

The unique thing about puzzles is that until the last word, number, or piece is put into place, the puzzle is incomplete. Every word, number, or piece is needed. Likewise, every member of this organization is essential. If one person fails to attend a meeting or function, a piece of this club is missing making it incomplete.

Tonight, the officers of the _____ (name of club) will be installed using pieces of a jigsaw puzzle. Each officer has different duties to perform just as each piece of a puzzle is shaped differently. The officers are the leadership pieces in this organization. They provide guidance and help to keep everything running smoothly. Will the newly officers please come forward? (Have officers line up in order with the treasurer first.)

The treasurer's piece in the puzzle is a financial piece. Your duties include collecting and depositing money, writing checks, and giving a monthly financial statement to your club. Do you accept the responsibilities of this office? (The officer should answer, "I do." Give the officer a puzzle piece and small puzzle.) Congratulations. You are an important piece in this organization. Always work to keep your club complete.

———————#———————

The corresponding secretary's piece in the puzzle is an inscribing piece. Your duties include writing letters and notes that will display your club in a positive light to the community. Do you accept the responsibilities of this office? (The officer should answer, "I do." Give the officer a puzzle piece and small puzzle.) Congratulations. You are an important piece in this organization. Always work to keep your club complete.

———————#———————

The secretary's piece in the puzzle is a writing piece. Your duties include taking minutes at every meeting and making sure that all the decisions of your club are accurately recorded for the club's history. Do you accept the responsibilities of this office? (The officer should answer, "I do." Give the officer a puzzle piece and small puzzle.) Congratulations. You are an important piece in this organization. Always work to keep your club complete.

The second vice-president's piece in the puzzle is the program piece. Your duties include chairing and guiding the program committee so that the programs selected meet the diverse needs of your membership. Do you accept the responsibilities of this office? (The officer should answer, "I do." Give the officer a puzzle piece and small puzzle.) Congratulations. You are an important piece in this organization. Always work to keep your club complete.

The first vice-president's piece in the puzzle is the membership piece. Your duties include chairing the membership committee and working closely with your president. Spark club interest in all members, old and new, and support you president. Do you accept the responsibilities of this office? (The officer should answer, "I do." Give the officer a puzzle piece and small puzzle.) Congratulations. You are an important piece in this organization. Always work to keep your club complete.

The president's piece in the puzzle is the leadership piece. Your duties include presiding at all meetings, appointing committees and chairmen, giving members encouragement, following up on all club matters, and representing your club within the community. You have been given the highest honor your club can bestow. Serve your membership with love and loyalty. Do you accept the responsibilities of this office? (The officer should answer, "I do." Give the officer a puzzle piece and empty puzzle box.) Congratulations. You are an important piece in this organization. Always work to keep your club complete.

On the table is an unfinished jigsaw puzzle. It represents the members of the _____ (name of club). Currently, it is incomplete. It needs the officers' pieces to be whole. (To the officers.) Would you please place your pieces in the puzzle? (Continue once the officers are finished.) Officers, you have now assumed your positions within this organization; however, you are not the only pieces in this club.

(To the membership.) Members, you are the other pieces needed to complete this club. Just as every piece in a puzzle fits snugly together to make a picture, every member of this organization is joined together to accomplish club goals. Support one another, and your club will be able to achieve great success.

Key Capers

Individuals generally have an assortment of keys, all of which are necessary and play an important part in daily living. Organizations are comprised of many different kinds of people, all of which are essential and become a vital part of a club's life. In this ceremony, keys are used to illustrate the distinctive duties of each club's officer. Keys provide access to many things, such as homes, cars, and safety deposit boxes. In the same manner, officers provide leadership to a group and help members achieve club goals.

A remembrance for each officer would be a key that is decorated with a piece of ribbon. Six keys are needed. Since each office has unique duties, the keys should differ in either size, shape, or color. New keys can be purchased at a hardware store. Used keys can be found at a garage sale, flea market, rummage sale, or even at a hardware store. Stores sometimes have incorrectly ground keys, and they might give them to you free of charge. If you have some old keys that you do not need any more, use them. The ribbon can be any color, or colors. It should be between 8- to 12-inches in length and no more than one-half inch in width. Thread the ribbon through the key's top hole, and tie it together into a bow, or knot. Ribbon can be bought at a craft store, a fabric store, or a florist's. Preparation time includes finding and buying the keys, purchasing the ribbon, and decorating the keys with the ribbon. Cost for this idea varies depending on whether you buy new or used keys. Ribbon is inexpensive.

A second choice is to give each officer a key that has a key chain attached to it. Six keys and key chains are needed. The keys, which represent the distinctive duties of each officer, should be different either in size, shape, or color. Use any kind of key you can find. Key chains can be found at gift stores, discount department stores, and drug stores. It is not necessary that all six chains be identical. The key chains could also be engraved with the club's name, or title of the office, if the budget permits. Price of this suggestion depends on the key chains selected, and whether or not they are engraved. Preparation time includes obtaining the keys, finding appropriate key chains, attaching the chains to the keys, and engraving the key chains, if that is so desired.

This ceremony lasts about 10 minutes and could be used for any club, especially a men's organization. A light ceremony, it would suit any students' group, too. Students can identify with keys since they are more than likely to possess a house key and have, or want, their own set of car keys. If this service is used for a men's club, or a student group that has young men in it, do not decorate the keys with frilly ribbon. Prepare the script and gifts in advance. Script preparation includes telling the officers before the ceremony that they will be required to answer an installation question with the words, "I do."

Installation Ceremony

Keys are essential to our daily lives and serve a variety of purposes. Some functions include starting cars, opening locked doors, providing access to a safety deposit box, and undoing a set of handcuffs. Likewise, officers are important to an organization and perform many tasks. One officer pays bills, another chairs the program committee, and another presides at club meetings.

Tonight the officers of the _____ (name of club) will be installed using a theme of keys. Each key used in this ceremony is different just as each office in this organization is distinct. Will the newly elected officers please come forward? (Have the officers line up in order with the treasurer first.)

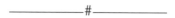

(Hold up the first key.) This is the key of the treasurer whose duties include balancing this club's checkbook, writing checks, collecting and depositing money, and giving monthly financial statements. (To the officer.) As the new treasurer, do you promise to fulfill all the duties of this office? (The officer should answer, "I do.") May this key unlock your potential and help you be productive. (Give the key to the officer.)

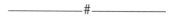

(Hold up the second key.) This is the key of the corresponding secretary whose duties include writing letters, answering mail, and helping this club shine in the public eye. (To the officer.) As the new corresponding secretary, do you promise to fulfill all the duties of this office? (The officer should answer, "I do.") May this key unlock your potential and help you be productive. (Give the key to the officer.)

(Hold up the third key.) This is the key of the secretary whose duties include listening attentively, writing quickly and accurately, and producing clear and precise minutes. (To the officer.) As the new secretary, do you promise to fulfill all the duties of this office? (The officer should answer, "I do.") May this key unlock your potential and help you be productive. (Give the key to the officer.)

————————#————————

(Hold up the fourth key.) This is the key of the second vice-president whose duties include chairing the program committee and helping the president. Guide your committee in their selection of programs so that the line-up will be of interest to your diverse membership. (To the officer.) As the new second vice-president, do you promise to fulfill all the duties of this office? (The officer should answer, "I do.") May this key unlock your potential and help you be productive. (Give the key to the officer.)

(Hold up the fifth key.) This is the key of the first vice-president whose duties will include chairing the membership committee and working closely with the president. Work to keep all members, old and new, interested in club projects, and take time to learn about your organization's policies and procedures. (To the officer.) As the new first vice-president, do you promise to fulfill all the duties of this office? (The officer should answer, "I do.") May this key unlock your potential and help you be productive. (Give the key to the officer.)

(Hold up the sixth key.) This is the key of the president whose duties include presiding at all meetings, appointing strong committees and proper chairmen, following up on club details, and supporting all club functions. You are now this club's leader and representative to the community. Make your members proud. (To the officer.) As the new president, do you promise to fulfill all the duties of this office? (The officer should answer, "I do.") May this key unlock your potential and help you be productive. (Give the key to the officer.)

(To the membership.) Members, you are the other key elements in this club. You possess many skills and abilities that make this organization complete. Unlock your potential and help your club be productive.

Flying High

A favorite pastime of all ages, kites can be found in many different sizes, shapes, and colors. However, in order for a kite to fly, climb, and soar high into the sky, it needs the wind. Clubs can be compared to kites. Memberships are made up of all types of people who bring various skills, talents and abilities to an organization. In order for a club to run efficiently and reach new heights, it needs capable officers to lead and direct. These leaders become the group's support just as the wind is a kite's support.

A gift suggestion for each officer would be a colorful kite. Kites can be purchased at a toy store, a discount department store, or through mail order catalogs, especially those featuring children's learning toys. They do not have to be identical in size, shape, or color since the duties of each officer are not the same. Six kites are needed for the ceremony. This gift would be low-priced. A trip to the store to buy the kites is the only preparation time required. Depending on the season, kites may not be out in the stores with the other merchandise. If you do not see any kites in the store, ask a manager if they are available. Allot yourself additional preparation time if you order kites through a catalog.

Another alternative is to make an origami kite for each officer. Books on origami, or Japanese paper art, can be found at your local library, a bookstore, or, sometimes, larger craft stores. Follow the directions given in the book. It might take some time to perfect the art, so be patient. Because the kites should be bright and colorful, use either origami paper, or vividly designed wrapping paper designs.

Origami paper can be found at craft stores. Wrapping paper can be found at discount department stores and card and gift stores. This idea requires time to make six kites; however, it has the advantage of being reasonable in cost.

This ceremony last about 10 minutes. It is a lighthearted ceremony that can be used for any organization, but would lend itself well to a students' group, or a sports and leisure club. It is also appropriate for an educational association since these groups attempt to get students to soar to new heights. Make certain that the script and gifts are prepared in advance. Preparation of the script includes obtaining the new officers' names since they are used in the ceremony. Also, inform the officers prior to the ceremony that they will be required to answer an installation question with the words, "I do."

INSTALLATION CEREMONY

Kites have been around for centuries and are a favorite pastime of all ages. They are flown for scientific and military purposes, competitions, and pure pleasure. Kites can be found in many different colors, sizes, shapes, and designs. Like kites, clubs are comprised of various kinds of people who bring diverse skills, talents, and abilities to an organization.

Tonight the officers of the _____ (name of club) will be installed using a theme of kites. A kite needs a breeze to soar high into the sky. So too, an organization needs officers to help reach club goals. The officers can be compared to the wind as they lead, guide, and support the membership. Will the newly elected officers please come forward? (Have the officers line up in order with the treasurer first.)

—————————#—————————

_____ (name of treasurer), you have been elected to serve as treasurer. Your duties include collecting all dues and monies, making deposits, writing checks, and giving monthly financial statements. Do you promise to carry out your duties? (Officer should answer, "I do." Give the officer a kite.) May this kite help you soar to new heights as you fulfill all the obligations of your office.

—————————#—————————

_____ (name of corresponding secretary), you have been elected to serve as corresponding secretary. Your duties include writing notes and letters, and promoting your club in a favorable fashion. Do you promise to carry out your duties? (Officer should answer, "I do." Give the officer a kite.) May this kite help you soar to new heights as you fulfill all the obligations of your office.

—————————#—————————

_____ (name of secretary), you have been elected to serve as secretary. Your duties include taking minutes at all meetings and keeping an accurate record of your club's business. Do you promise to carry out your duties? (Officer should answer, "I do." Give the officer a kite.) May this kite help you soar to new heights as you fulfill all the obligations of your office.

—————————#—————————

_____ (name of second vice-president), you have been elected to serve as second vice-president. Your duties include chairing the program committee and being ready to assume any other duties that your president may assign you. Do you promise to carry out your duties? (Officer should answer, "I do." Give the officer a kite.) May this kite help you soar to new heights as you fulfill all the obligations of your office.

—————————#—————————

_____ (name of first vice-president), you have been elected to serve as first vice-president. Your duties include chairing the membership committee, assisting the president, and becoming knowledgeable of all your club's policies and procedures. Do you promise to carry out your duties? (Officer should answer, "I do." Give the officer a kite.) May this kite help you soar to new heights as you fulfill all the obligations of your office.

—————#—————

_____ (name of president), you have been elected to serve as president. Your duties include presiding at all meetings, appointing chairmen and committees, and keeping up on all club business. Your club has bestowed upon you its highest honor. Make your membership proud. Do you promise to carry out your duties? (Officer should answer, "I do." Give the officer a kite.) May this kite help you soar to new heights as you fulfill the obligations of your office.

—————#—————

(To the membership.) Members, your officers have now been installed. However, they cannot work alone. You, also, are an important part of this organization. The talents, skills, and abilities that you bring to this club are greatly treasured and needed. Just as a kite is held to the earth by a string, your club is held together by the support of its membership. Working together, your club will be able to soar to new heights.

Grand Opening

Letter openers are valuable tools that open envelopes quickly and efficiently. By using an opener, a person is saved from getting a paper cut, and the contents within an envelope are rescued from being ripped. Officers of an organization can be compared to letter openers. Principal leaders within a club, the officers are called upon to perform their distinctive duties promptly and effectively. The fulfillment of their obligations alleviates the membership from disruption and worry. Officers help keep an organization running smoothly just as a letter opener smoothly opens an envelope.

A letter opener is the perfect gift. Six openers are needed, and they can be the same, or different, depending on your preference. Gift stores, Christian bookstores, and mail order catalogs generally carry letter openers. This idea requires time to locate six openers. They might need to be ordered, especially if you want identical ones, so begin looking for them several weeks, or months, prior to the ceremony. Letter openers range in price, but this suggestion could be quite expensive.

This ceremony runs about 10 minutes in length and is appropriate for any organization. The theme is most fitting for educational groups which help to open students' minds and religious organizations which help to open people's hearts. This service would also be most appropriate for an historical society, or a men's organization. The script and gifts should be prepared in advance. Preparation of the script includes informing the new officers, before the ceremony, that they will be required to answer an installation question with the words, "Yes, I do."

INSTALLATION CEREMONY

Letter openers are used to open sealed envelopes quickly and efficiently. In addition to this convenience, an opener can save a person from getting a paper cut, and it can prevent an envelope's contents from being torn. All of these factors make a letter opener an extremely handy and helpful tool.

Officers are beneficial to a club. When they promptly and proficiently perform their many duties and tasks, they contribute to an organization's stability and relieve members from stress and anxiety. Officers who are competent at their jobs help a club flourish.

Tonight, the officers of the _____ (name of club) will be installed with letter openers. The openers symbolize each officer's willingness to become a leader within this organization. As they assume their new leadership roles, the officers also promise to fulfill their many new duties. Will the newly elected officers please come forward? (Have the officers line up in order with the treasurer first.)

(Give letter opener to treasurer.) The treasurer opens this club's bank statements. Other duties include writing checks, depositing money, and giving a monthly financial statement to your club. Do you promise to fulfill the many obligations of this office? (Officer should answer, "Yes, I do.") May your letter opener remind you of your new responsibilities.

(Give letter opener to corresponding secretary.) The corresponding secretary opens this club's correspondence. Other duties include writing letters and notes, and promoting your club in a favorable fashion. Do you promise to fulfill the many obligations of this office? (Officer should answer, "Yes, I do.") May your letter opener remind you of your new responsibilities.

(Give letter opener to secretary.) The secretary opens this club's books. Other duties include taking minutes at every meeting and keeping the club's historical records. Do you promise to fulfill the many obligations of this office? (Officer should answer, "Yes, I do.") May your letter opener remind you of your new responsibilities.

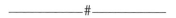

(Give letter opener to second vice-president.) The second vice-president opens valuable mail about programs. Other duties include chairing the program committee and assisting the president. Do you promise to fulfill the many obligations of this office? (Officer should answer, "Yes, I do.") May your letter opener remind you of your new responsibilities.

(Give letter opener to first vice-president.) The first vice-president opens important information about membership. Other duties include keeping the membership excited and informed about club business, and working closely with the president who will rely on you for help and support. Do you promise to fulfill the many obligations of this office? (Officer should answer, "Yes, I do.") May your letter opener remind you of your new responsibilities.

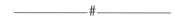

(Give letter opener to president.) The president opens all of this club's official mail. Other duties include presiding at meetings, appointing committees and chairmen, following up on club matters to see that they are being done properly and on time, encouraging fellow members, and representing your club. Do you promise to fulfill the many obligations of this office? (Officer should answer, "Yes, I do.") May your letter opener remind you of your new responsibilities.

(To the membership.) Members, you also have important duties to perform. You must support and encourage your new officers as you work with them to achieve your club's many goals. Letter openers smoothly open envelopes, and they are an efficient tool. Likewise, when members and officers work together, they keep their club running smoothly, and make it an effective organization.

Best Seller

In this ceremony, officers and members of a club are compared to the components of a book. Although certain parts of a book provide guidance for a reader, every page is needed in order to have a complete work. Similarly, the officers of an organization supply leadership and direction, but every member is needed to establish and meet club goals. Every element of a book and every member of a club is important and essential.

An inspirational book is a nice keepsake of the event. Identical, or different, books can be given. This idea requires a trip to a bookstore and time to browse. If you choose to give each officer the same book, the books might need to be ordered. Allow for this possibility, and start looking weeks before the ceremony. If you decide to give each officer a different book, not as much time is required in advance. Prior to the ceremony, mark each officer's book so that it can be opened to the appropriate page mentioned during the installation. Identify page numbers for the treasurer, the index for the secretary, the table of contents for the second vice-president, the title page for the first vice-president, and the cover for the president. When selecting a book, or books, make certain that the above elements are included. This suggestion could be high priced depending on the books selected. Preparation includes a trip, or trips, to a bookstore and time to pre-mark the books.

Another possibility is to give each officer a bookmark. If this option is chosen, one book will still be needed. Go to a bookstore and buy an inspirational book that can be given as an additional gift to the incoming president following the installation. Specific elements in the book should be marked for use during the ceremony. Identify page numbers for the treasurer, the index for the secretary, the table of contents for the second vice-president, and the title page for the first vice-president. The cover represents the president. The bookmarks given to the incoming officers can be used to mark the above places. The six bookmarks need not be identical and can be purchased at a bookstore, a gift shop, or a discount department store. Preparation includes buying the bookmarks and the president's book and marking the book prior to the ceremony. This suggestion has the advantage of being reasonable in cost.

This ceremony will last about 10 minutes. Although it could be used for any organization, it is best suited for an educational association, a literary society, or a religious group. Make certain that the script and gifts are ready in advance. Preparation of the script should include obtaining the new officers' names since they are used in the ceremony. Also, if bookmarks are given as gifts, substitute "bookmark" for "book" where it is appropriate.

INSTALLATION CEREMONY

Books are an important part of our daily lives. Encyclopedias give us information; cookbooks assist us with recipes; self-help books teach us how to improve ourselves; and novels provide us with escape and entertainment. Whatever subject you can think of, there is a book out there about it.

A club can be compared to a book. Just as there are many elements in a book, there are many facets in a club. Within a book, one can find a title page, a table of contents, and page numbers. Likewise, within a club, one can find members that possess administrative skills, creative talents, and leadership qualities. Each part of a book is essential to make it complete. So too, every member of a club is necessary to make it whole.

Tonight, the officers of the _____ (name of club) will be installed using the various parts of a book. A gift of a book (book-mark) will be presented to them as they are installed. Will the officers to be installed please come forward? (Have the officers line up in order with the treasurer first.)

——————#——————

(Open book to the pre-marked page number.) Page numbers are an important part of any book. _____ (name of officer), as treasurer, numbers will become a significant part of your club life. Your duties include writing checks, collecting dues, and giving monthly financial statements to your club.

Just as page numbers help one know where one is in a book, your numbers shall help the membership know where your club is financially. Congratulations on your new office. (Give the gift to the officer.)

——————#——————

(Open book to the pre-marked index.) When looking for a particular place in a book, the index is a recommended starting point. _____ (name of officer), as secretary, you will be a source of information for your club. Your duties include recording your club's decisions and keeping its history.

Just as an index is used to help find something quickly in a book, your minutes shall help members find out about your club's past actions. Congratulations on your new office. (Give the gift to the officer.)

——————#——————

(Open book to the pre-marked table of contents.) Another part of a book that presents useful information is the table of contents. _____ (name of officer), as second vice-president, you will be acquiring leadership knowledge. Your duties include chairing the program committee and assisting the president.

Just as a table of contents tells a reader what a book contains, you will be telling your members what kind of programs the upcoming year holds. Congratulations on your new office. (Give the gift to the officer.)

—————#—————

(Open book to the pre-marked title page.) The first page in a book is called the title page. _____ (name of officer), as first vice-president, you will be the understudy to the president. Your duties include chairing the membership committee and working closely with your president.

Just as the title page of a book provides publication information, you will communicate club knowledge to your membership. Keep up on all club matters, read the constitution and by-laws, and share what you know with the membership. Congratulations on your new office. (Give the gift to the officer.)

—————#—————

(Hold up a book to show its cover.) When looking at a book, the first thing one sees is the cover. _____ (name of officer), as president, you are this club's leader and their representative to the community. You are what people will see first. Your duties include presiding at all meetings, appointing committees and chairmen, following up on club details, and providing encouragement to members.

Just as the cover of a book protects the pages within, you must encompass and protect the members within your club. Love and care for your club's membership. And remember, that a book well worn is a book well-loved. Congratulations on your new office. (Give the gift to the officer.)

—————#—————

The officers are now installed; however, the most important part of the book has not been mentioned—the pages. (To the membership.) You, the members of the _____ (name of club), are the pages of this book. Without you, there would not be a club. Just as every page of a book is essential for a reader, every member of this organization is needed to accomplish your club goals. Officers and members, support one another so that when you conclude this next club year, you will be able to say, "This is the best book our club has ever written."

It Is Written

Pens are used in this ceremony to illustrate how people leave a mark on those around them. Actions, words, and deeds become the pages that are written for others to read. Important leaders of an organization, the officers need to write positive pages for their membership and community to read. These affirmative pages, a chapter in the club's history, are composed when the officers fulfill the various tasks and duties of their respective positions.

A pen that has been decorated with ribbon and baby's breath makes an appropriate gift. Give nicer pens, not the cheap throw away pens that come eight or ten in a package. Six pens are needed, but they do not all have to be the same in color, or design. Nicer pens can be purchased in discount department stores, card and gift stores, and office supply stores. Ribbon and baby's breath add a decorative touch to the pens. Use ribbon that does not exceed one-half inch in width. Length is determined by the size of the bow and streamers that you want on the pen. Any color, or design, of ribbon can be used. However, if the pens have a pattern on them, a solid colored ribbon would work best. A small sprig of baby's breath can be placed onto the ribbon right before the single bow is made. Ribbon and baby's breath can be found at a craft store, or a florist's. Not much of either item is required. Remember to give yourself enough time to purchase the necessary supplies and then decorate the pens. Cost will vary according to what type of pens are bought, but it should be reasonable.

This light ceremony runs between 10 and 15 minutes. Appropriate for any club, this theme would lend itself well to a literary group, an educational association, or an historical society. It is also a proper service for a men's organization; however, if used for a men's group, you might not want to decorate the pens. Preparation of the script includes obtaining the new officer's names since they are used in the ceremony. Also, make sure that the gifts are ready prior to the day of the service.

INSTALLATION CEREMONY

Aware of it or not, each of us writes a page for others to see. Some people write pages of love, understanding, and cheerfulness while others write pages that are filled with hatred, intolerance, and bitterness. Our actions, words, and deeds become our compositions.

Officers of an organization are no exception. Together, they write an entire chapter in their club's history. To ensure that the pages written are positive, the officers must strive to complete their various obligations promptly and effectively. A successful club is comprised of dedicated leaders.

Tonight, the officers of the _____ (name of club) will be given a pen as they are installed. These pens can contribute to the writing of this club's next chapter when the officers use them to fulfill the duties and tasks of their respective positions. Will the newly elected officers please come forward? (Have the officers line up in order with the treasurer first.)

———————#———————

(Give the pen to the treasurer.) _____ (name of officer), as treasurer, your pen will be signing checks, balancing the checkbook, and making out treasurer's reports. Some of your other duties include collecting dues and paying bills. The page that you write is in the world of money management. It is a page that will keep members informed as to this club's financial status. Congratulations, and may your mark always be in the black.

——————#——————

(Give the pen to the corresponding secretary.) _____ (name of officer), as corresponding secretary, your pen will be writing letters, responding to correspondence, and making notations on incoming mail. The page that you write is in the world of communication. It is a page that will keep members, and the community, informed as to this club's happenings. Congratulations, and may your mark always be in bold script.

——————#——————

(Give the pen to the secretary.) _____ (name of officer), as secretary, your pen will be constantly taking minutes at executive board meetings and general club meetings. Your minutes are the records of your club, and you are the keeper of the records. The page that you write is in the world of history. It is a page that will remind members of their club's votes and decisions. Congratulations, and may your mark always be precise.

——————#——————

(Give the pen to the second vice-president.) _____ (name of officer), as second vice-president, your pen will be writing down program ideas and suggestions. Some of your duties include chairing the program committee, learning about your club's policies and procedures, and familiarizing yourself with the by-laws. The page that you write is in the world of information and entertainment. It is a page that will generate the interest among your membership for upcoming club programs. Congratulations, and may your mark always be exciting.

——————#——————

(Give the pen to the first vice-president.) _____ (name of officer), as first vice-president, your pen will be signing new membership applications, keeping a list of ideas for future club projects, and writing words of encouragement to fellow club members. Some of your duties include chairing the membership committee and working closely with your president. The page that you write is in the world of growth. It is a page that will challenge members to add to their club's numbers. Congratulations, and may your mark always be enthusiastic.

——————#——————

(Give the pen to the president.) _____ (name of officer), as president, your pen will be writing agendas, taking notes, following up on details, making lists, and appointing committees. At times, your pen may never cease to write as you fulfill your many obligations. You must be tactful, courteous, conscientious, and always loyal to your office and your membership. The page that you write is in the world of development. It is a page that will inspire members to reach beyond their past to a new future. Congratulations, and may your mark always be one of encouragement.

——————#——————

(To the membership.) Although the officers have been given pens, they do not write the club's next chapter alone. Everyone within an organization contributes to the writing process, page by page, year by year. Members, work with your officers and support them, so that the chapter composed during this next administration is the best chapter your club has ever written.

Quotables

Famous sayings are often quoted to inspire and challenge people. Frequently heard at weddings, commencements, and church services, quotations make an excellent backdrop for an installation ceremony. Officers need to hear words of encouragement as they assume their new leadership positions within their club. Once they feel capable of completing their various job requirements, they are better able to inspire and motivate other club members to achieve their potentials.

As a remembrance of the event, give each officer a copy of their particular quote. Purchase drawing paper, or parchment paper, at an art supply, or craft store. Using a black felt-tip marker, write each quote out on a piece of paper. If you can do calligraphy, or know someone who can, write the quotes in that style. The quotes could also be printed on a personal computer using a script font. Once the ink dries, the quotes can either be framed, or given as they are. If parchment paper is used, they could also be rolled up and tied with a ribbon. Frames can be purchased at a discount department store, or a craft store. Use either 8-inch by 11-inch frames, or 5-inch by 7-inch frames, depending on the size of your paper. The quotes could also be matted with black mats. Any style and size of ribbon could be used if you decide to roll up the paper. Amount of preparation time varies according to how elaborate you decide to make these gifts. Give yourself enough time to write out the quotes and allow the ink to dry before you frame or roll them up. If done on a computer, allow time to design and print out the quotes. Cost for this suggestion would be minimal if you decide to give out the quotes as they are, or roll them up with ribbon. The price will increase if you decide to purchase mats and frames.

You might give each officer a set of homemade stationery with their specific quote as the heading. Purchase a ream of white paper and plain white envelopes. Both items can be found at an office supply store. Using a personal computer, select a script font, type in the quote, and print it on a piece of paper. Remember to include the author's name with the quote. After printing, make at least a dozen copies for the officer. Put the correct number of envelopes with the new letterhead, and tie each bundle with colored ribbon. Ribbon can be found at a craft store, or a florist's and can be any color, or design. Select ribbon that is about one-half inch wide. Cut the ribbon long enough so that it can be tied in a bow in the front of the stationery bundle. This idea requires time to purchase paper and envelopes; design, print, and copy the quotes; and arrange the new stationery into bundles. Although it demands a time commitment, it has the advantage of being economical in cost.

This ceremony is about 15 minutes in length. A solemn service, it can be used for any organization, but would work well for an historical society, or a literary group. Make certain that the gifts and script are ready in advance. Preparation of the script includes informing the new officers that they will be required to answer an installation question with the words, "I do."

INSTALLATION CEREMONY

Throughout the centuries famous sayings by men and women have been recorded for posterity. Slivers of wisdom, these quotations are often repeated in an effort to inspire, comfort, and encourage others. Quotes challenge people to reach higher goals and dream greater dreams.

Officers of an organization need inspiration and encouragement to face the challenges of their new positions. Once they learn how to successfully perform their tasks, they are better able to help other members fulfill their duties. Effective leadership motivates others to be their best as they strive to attain their goals and realize their dreams.

Tonight, the officers of the _____ (name of club) will be installed with famous quotations. Officers, may these quotes challenge you to complete your duties efficiently, and inspire you to serve your membership with enthusiasm. Will the newly elected officers please come forward? (Have the officers line up in order with the treasurer first.)

Ralph Waldo Emerson once said, "Pay every debt as if God wrote the bill." The treasurer of a club pays the bills. You must settle your club's accounts promptly. Other duties include collecting dues, depositing money, and giving a monthly financial report to your club. Do you promise to fulfill the new challenges set before you? (The officer should answer, "I do.")

May Emerson's quote provide you with inspiration and encouragement as you work to achieve club goals and dream new dreams. (Give the gift to the officer.) Best wishes in the year ahead.

Benjamin Franklin said, "Do not squander time; for that's the stuff life is made of." The corresponding secretary of a club spends a great deal of time on correspondence. You must learn to manage the minutes of your day wisely. Your duties include answering letters, writing notes, and promoting your club in a favorable fashion. Do you promise to fulfill the new challenges set before you? (The officer should answer, "I do.")

May Franklin's quote provide you with inspiration and encouragement as you work to achieve club goals and dream new dreams. (Give the gift to the officer.) Best wishes in the year ahead.

Dante (DAHN tay) Alighieri (ah lee GYA ree) said, "He listens well who takes notes." The secretary of a club takes many notes. You must be able to listen well in order to take accurate minutes. Your duties include taking minutes at every meeting and keeping the club's historical records. Do you promise to fulfill the new challenges set before you? (The officer should answer, "I do.")

May Dante's quote provide you with inspiration and encouragement as you work to achieve club goals and dream new dreams. (Give the gift to the officer.) Best wishes in the year ahead.

John F. Kennedy said, "Leadership and learning are indispensable to each other." The second vice-president of a club is a leader in training. In this office, you will be learning about your club's policies and procedures. Your duties include chairing the program committee, solving program problems, and assisting the president when needed. Do you promise to fulfill the new challenges set before you? (The officer should answer, "I do.")

May Kennedy's quote provide you with inspiration and encouragement as you work to achieve club goals and dream new dreams. (Give the gift to the officer.) Best wishes in the year ahead.

Eleanor Roosevelt said, "You gain strength, courage, and confidence by every experience in which you really stop to look fear in the face. You are able to say to yourself, 'I lived through this horror, I can take the next thing that comes along.' ...You must do the thing you think you cannot do." The first vice-president of a club is in training for the presidency. You must learn to handle situations, especially those you think you cannot do. Your duties include chairing the membership committee, keeping club members informed of all club projects and functions, and working closely with your president. Do you promise to fulfill the new challenges set before you? (The officer should answer, "I do.")

May Roosevelt's quote provide you with inspiration and encouragement as you work to achieve club goals and dream new dreams. (Give the gift to the officer.) Best wishes in the year ahead.

Theodore Roosevelt once said, "The best executive is the one who has sense enough to pick good men to do what he wants done, and self-restraint enough to keep from meddling with them while they do it." The president is a club's chief executive. You must be able to delegate, and, then, let members do their jobs. Giving members this freedom, allows creativity to flow and new ideas to be born. Your duties include presiding at meetings, appointing chairmen and committees, and representing the club at community functions. Do you promise to fulfill the new challenges set before you? (The officer should answer, "I do.")

May Roosevelt's quote provide you with inspiration and encouragement as you work to achieve club goals and dream new dreams. (Give the gift to the officer.) Best wishes in the year ahead.

(To the membership.) Robert F. Kennedy once said, "Some men see things as they are and say, why. I dream things that never were and say, why not." Members, you also have responsibilities. Your duties include supporting your officers, attending meetings, and working at club events. Never be satisfied with seeing things as they are, but look for ways to make them better. May Kennedy's quote provide you with inspiration and encouragement as you work with your officers to achieve club goals and dream new dreams.

Grand Gourmet

Recipe ingredients provide an excellent parallel to clubs. In a recipe, every ingredient is significant to the outcome of a dish. In an organization, every officer and member is essential for the achievement of goals. Officers are an integral part of a club's leadership, and they have specific duties to perform which help to keep a group running smoothly. If one ingredient in a recipe is forgotten, the result can be disastrous. Likewise, the failure of an officer to fulfill the tasks of a particular office can create a club disaster.

One gift idea is to give each officer a recipe and a set of measuring cups, or measuring spoons. Copy down one of your favorite recipes onto six recipe cards. The finished cards can be placed inside the measuring cups. If you decide to use measuring spoons, punch a hole in each card and attach it with a ribbon through the center holes in the measuring spoons. Recipe cards can be purchased at a discount department store, a kitchen store, or a gift store. Measuring cups and spoons can be found at a discount department store, a kitchen store, or a grocery store. If you decide to give spoons, use curly ribbon for attaching the cards. Pieces of ribbon should be cut about 8-inches in length. Ribbon is available at card stores and discount department stores. The necessary kitchen items are generally inexpensive. Preparation time includes buying the necessary items, copying your recipe onto six cards, and putting the cards inside the cups, or attaching them to the spoons. If you do not have a recipe, use the following one for a "Successful Club." 2 cups of enthusiasm, 1 cup of support,

1 cup of responsibility, 2 tablespoons of dedication, 2 tablespoons of joy, and a pinch of flexibility. Mix gently until club goals are achieved. Then add one pound of happiness. Stir and watch a successful club year unfold.

A cookbook as a gift is another option. Six books are needed. It is not necessary that all of the books be identical. Time will be needed to go to a bookstore and browse if this gift idea is selected. Besides bookstores, cookbooks can also be found at checkout counters in grocery stores and discount department stores. Cost for this suggestion varies depending on what kind of cookbooks are purchased.

This ceremony is a lighthearted one that lasts between 10 and 15 minutes. It is best suited for any women's organization, especially a group that is interested in cooking. If books are given, this service would also be appropriate for a literary society. Make certain that the script and gifts are prepared in advance.

INSTALLATION CEREMONY

All of us have recipes. Some are family ones that have been passed down for generations. Some are newer ones that we have found in magazines and books. And some are fat-free. According to Webster's Dictionary, a recipe is "a list of materials and directions needed for preparing a dish." The list of materials is very important. Just ask anyone who has ever forgotten an ingredient. The result can be disastrous.

Tonight, the officers of the _____ (name of club) will be installed using a recipe theme. Just as a recipe has certain ingredients that must be included in order for a dish to be perfect, each officer has certain duties that must be performed in order for a club to have success. The officers are vital ingredients and help members accomplish club goals. Will the newly elected officers please come forward at this time? (Have the officers line up in order with the treasurer first.)

The treasurer adds a cup of financial security to this club. Your duties include signing checks, collecting and depositing money, and giving monthly financial statements. Your job is important and provides an essential ingredient to your club. The fulfillment of your duties will result in a delicious club year for all members. (Give the gift to the officer.)

The corresponding secretary adds a dash of spice to this club. Your duties include writing letters and notes, answering mail, and promoting your club within the community. Your job is important and provides an essential ingredient to your club. The completion of your duties will result in a tasteful club year for all members. (Give the gift to the officer.)

The secretary adds a tablespoon of accuracy to this club. Your duties include taking minutes at all meetings, recording all business and actions, and keeping the club's historical records. Your job is important and provides an essential ingredient to your club. The realization of your duties will result in an appetizing club year for all members. (Give the gift to the officer.)

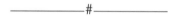

The second vice-president adds a pint of information to this club. Your duties include chairing the program committee and being prepared for the unexpected. Your job is important and provides an essential ingredient to your club. The performance of your duties will result in a savory club year for all members. (Give the gift to the officer.)

The first vice-president adds a heap of enthusiasm to this club. Your duties include chairing the membership committee and working closely with the president. Your job is important and provides an essential ingredient to your club. The accomplishment of your duties will result in a nourishing club year for all members. (Give the gift to the officer.)

The president adds ounces of love and leadership to the club. Your duties include presiding at all meetings, following up on club matters, appointing committees and chairmen, representing your club within the community, and listening to your members concerns. Your job is important and provides an essential ingredient to your club. The mastery of your duties will result in an aromatic and delectable club year for all members. (Give the gift to the officer.)

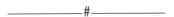

(To the membership.) The officers have now been installed for the upcoming year. However, you, the members of this club, are the final ingredients. You are the cups of support needed to make this club recipe a success. Your duties will be assisting your officers so that, together, you can make a most scrumptious club year.

The Good Book

In order to effectively lead an organization, officers need wisdom. "The Bible," an excellent source on the subject, provides appropriate scripture quotations for the installation of a club's officers. Leaders demonstrate wisdom when they successfully complete the many tasks and duties associated with their respective positions. With the acquisition of authentic wisdom, officers are able to properly guide and direct a club.

A book on wisdom would make a nice memento of the occasion. This idea necessitates a trip to a Christian bookstore to browse through their wisdom section. Although it would be nice to give six identical books, it is not necessary. Books might need to be ordered, so begin looking for them weeks, or months, in advance. Other than the time spent looking, or waiting for the books to arrive, this suggestion does not require any preparation. The cost can be moderate or expensive depending on the book, or books, you choose.

You might give each officer a bookmark that has a scripture verse about wisdom on it. Look for religious bookmarks at a Christian bookstore. The six bookmarks can be different, or the same, depending on your preference. This idea requires minimal time and is very low priced.

Another option is to give each officer a plaque that has a scripture verse about wisdom written on it. Christian bookstores carry these kind of plaques. Start looking months before the ceremony just in case the store does not have six plaques, and they need to be ordered.

It is your decision on whether or not all six should be identical. This suggestion requires time, especially if the plaques are not readily available. Like books, plaques can range from reasonably priced to high priced. This ceremony is about 15 minutes in length. A solemn ceremony, it could be used for any organization, but is best suited for a religious group. Select a gift option well in advance of the service so that the gifts are ready prior to the day of the installation. Also, make certain that the script is prepared.

INSTALLATION CEREMONY

Shortly after Solomon had become king of Israel, God appeared to him in a dream. I Kings, chapter 3 tells us that, in that dream, God asked Solomon what gift he would like. Solomon answered, "Give me the wisdom I need to rule your people with justice and to know the difference between good and evil. Otherwise, how would I ever be able to rule this great people of yours?" (Good News Bible, I Kings 3:9). God was pleased with Solomon's request, and He not only gave him the wisdom he asked for, but He also gave him great wealth and honor, more than any other king.

The officers of an organization must also seek wisdom in order to be effective leaders. Their offices have numerous duties, tasks and responsibilities, and they need to know how to successfully accomplish each one. In order for a club to flourish and grow, wise and dedicated leaders are an essential.

Tonight, the officers of the _____ (name of club) will be installed using different scriptural quotations about wisdom. Officers, as you search for God's wisdom, allow Him to guide you so that you, in turn, can provide guidance for your club. Will the newly elected officers please come forward? (Have the officers line up in order with the treasurer first.)

The treasurer's duties include collecting and depositing money, writing checks, and keeping accurate financial records. Proverbs 16:16 says, "It is better—much better—to have wisdom and knowledge than gold and silver." As treasurer, you handle your club's gold and silver. Learn how to manage it wisely. (Give the gift to the officer.) May God grant you wisdom to serve.

The corresponding secretary's duties include writing letters and taking care of correspondence. Proverbs 18:4 says, "A person's words can be a source of wisdom, deep as the ocean, fresh as a flowing stream." Your written words are what others, outside of your club, see. Keep your remarks fresh, like "a flowing stream." (Give the gift to the officer.) May God grant you wisdom to serve.

The secretary's duties include taking minutes at meetings and preserving your club's records. Proverbs 24:3 says, "Homes are built on the foundation of wisdom and understanding." Your minutes are part of the foundation of your club. Keep them accurate and precise. (Give the gift to the officer.) May God grant you wisdom to serve.

The second vice-president's duties include chairing and guiding the program committee so that a variety of programs are scheduled for the membership. Proverbs 3:18 says, "Those who become wise are happy; wisdom will give them life." Select programs that educate as well as entertain. Learning something new gives members an opportunity to enrich their lives and become wiser and happier. (Give the gift to the officer.) May God grant you wisdom to serve.

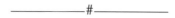

The first vice-president's duties include chairing the membership committee, working closely with your president, and learning about your club's by-laws, policies and procedures. Proverbs 4:5-6 says, "Get wisdom and insight!...Do not abandon wisdom, and she will protect you; love her, and she will keep you safe." You must strive to keep all members, old and new, informed about club functions. Do not abandon anyone, but love everyone. (Give the gift to the officer.) May God grant you wisdom to serve.

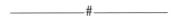

The president's duties include presiding at club meetings, appointing chairmen and committees, listening to club members, and representing your club within the community. Proverbs 4:7-9 says, "Getting wisdom is the most important thing you can do. Whatever else you get, get insight. Love wisdom, and she will make you great. Embrace her, and she will bring you honor. She will be your crowning glory." You must lead your membership with wisdom and insight. Your club will have a glorious and successful year if you embrace wisdom. (Give the gift to the officer.) May God grant you wisdom to serve.

(To the membership.) It takes wisdom to lead, but it also takes wisdom to follow. Members, you are called upon to support your new officers, attend meetings, and work on club projects. Do your tasks just as your officers do theirs. Proverbs 9:11 says, "Wisdom will add years to your life." As you support your officers, you are wisely adding years to your club's history and life. May God grant you wisdom to serve.

Stepping Out

There are many different kinds of shoes. Likewise, a club is comprised of various sorts of people. In this ceremony, shoes are used to represent the duties of each office. Just as a person wears a particular kind of shoe depending on the occasion, an officer performs certain tasks depending on the office. Shoes also provide support to the feet. In the same manner, when officers carry out their duties efficiently, they are giving their support to the club.

An appropriate gift for each officer is a pair of shoes. The shoes in the ceremony include a pair of jogging shoes, a pair of slippers, a pair of tap shoes, a pair of high heels, a pair of flats, and a pair of sandals. Buy used shoes since they will be cheaper than new ones. Second hand shoes can be found at thrift stores, rummage sales, garage sales, and flea markets. Because these shoes are only needed for the symbolism, it is suggested that a nicer gift, such as a potted flower or plant, also be given to each officer. If purchased second hand, the shoes will not be expensive, but it might take time to find the different kinds needed. The tap shoes may take the longest to find. Additional time could also be required to make the shoes presentable. Potted flowers and plants can be purchased at a florist's, a greenhouse, or a discount department store. Time is needed to buy the flowers or plants, but they are generally low in price.

The following ceremony will last between 10 and 15 minutes. Because this service uses women's shoes, it is best suited for a women's organization, or a young women's group, especially a civic club which would relate easily to being on the go. Make certain that the script and gifts are ready prior to the day of the installation. In preparing the script, obtain the new officers' names since they are used in the ceremony. Also, substitute the word "plant" for "flower" in the script if plants are being given instead of flowers.

INSTALLATION CEREMONY

Since prehistoric times, man has worn various forms of foot coverings which have evolved from leaves and barks to animal skins and leather. However, regardless of the material, the purpose of a pair of shoes has not changed. They provide support and protection to the feet. Likewise, officers of an organization give support and protection to their members. The competent performance of their duties helps their club run smoothly and keeps members free from worry.

Shoes can be found in many styles, colors, and name brands. Different kinds of shoes are designed for certain occasions. Some are meant for walking, others for dancing, and some are designed for evening apparel. One person's wardrobe might contain a dozen or more pairs of shoes.

Club officers also have distinctive duties to perform. One officer collects dues, one writes letters, and another presides at meetings.

Tonight, each officer will be installed with a pair of shoes that symbolizes the uniqueness of her particular office. The flower (plant) given with the shoes represents new beginnings for the officers and the club. Will the newly elected officers please come forward? (Have officers line up in order with the treasurer first.)

———————#———————

_____ (name of treasurer), you have been elected by your club to be the new treasurer. Your duties will include running to the bank to make deposits, running to meetings to collect dues and give financial statements, running to the post office to pay bills, and running to various other club functions with the checkbook, or money bag in hand.

(Give the gift to the officer.) May this pair of jogging shoes remind you of your new duties. Just as a pair of jogging shoes provides support and comfort to a runner's feet, the performance of your duties will provide financial security for your club. Congratulations and best wishes for a successful year.

———————#———————

_____ (name of corresponding secretary), you have been elected by your club to be the new corresponding secretary. Your duties will include writing letters and taking care of the club's correspondence. You are the liaison between your club and the community. It is your job to maintain your club's good public image.

(Give the gift to the officer.) May this pair of slippers remind you of your new duties. Slippers are soft, heelless shoes that provide comfort to their wearer. Your duties must be performed quietly and make life easy for the rest of the membership. Congratulations and best wishes for a successful year.

———————#———————

_____ (name of secretary), you have been elected by your club to be the new secretary. Your duties will include writing up accurate minutes of each meeting and keeping all the records of this club. Your pen will always be busy, not missing a beat, as you jot down words and actions.

(Give the gift to the officer.) May this pair of tap shoes remind you of your new duties. Just as a dancer uses tap shoes to make a clear, precise noise, the content of your minutes must always be clear and precise for the members of your club. Congratulations and best wishes for a successful year.

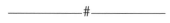

_____ (name of second vice-president), you have been elected by your club to be the new second vice-president. Your duties will include being the chairman of the program committee and assisting the president whenever needed. You shall acquire valuable leadership training in this new office.

(Give the gift to the officer.) May this pair of high heels remind you of your new duties. High heels come in various heights—high, low, and mid-sized. Like high heels, you will find that there are many kinds of programs. It will be your job to make sure that your committee selects a variety of programs for the membership. Congratulations and best wishes for a successful year.

—————————#—————————

_____ (name of first vice-president), you have been elected by your club to be the new first vice-president. Your duties will include being the chairman of the membership committee, as well as assisting the president. Get to know club members and make them feel important and comfortable within the organization. Keep them informed, inspired, and interested in all club business and projects. Lighten the president's load whenever possible, and support her. As the president's understudy, you are in an important year of leadership training.

(Give the gift to the officer.) May this pair of flats remind you of your new duties. Flats are twofold—they can be comfortable and dressy at the same time. Likewise, you will be filling two roles—one to the membership and one to the president. Congratulations and best wishes for a successful year.

—————————#—————————

_____ (name of president), you have been elected by your club to be the new president. Your duties will include presiding at meetings, appointing chairmen and committees, representing this club, and leading it. You must stay current on all matters and follow up on details. Encourage members and be available to them if problems arise. Serve your membership diligently for your club has given you its highest honor.

(Give the gift to the officer.) May this pair of sandals remind you of your new duties. Just as sandals allow air to circulate freely around the feet and toes, you must allow members to circulate freely within the club. Listen to your members, and you will be a good leader. Congratulations and best wishes for a successful year.

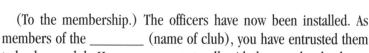

(To the membership.) The officers have now been installed. As members of the _____ (name of club), you have entrusted them to lead your club. However, you must walk with them as they lead you. You are the other pairs of shoes that are needed to make this club complete. Just as every pair of shoes has a distinct function, you have a definite purpose in this organization.

Support and protect your officers. Be quick to help, slow to blame, and heed the following Indian adage, "Grant that I may not criticize my neighbor until I have walked a mile in his moccasins."

Terrific Tokens

Officers of an organization have distinctive tasks to perform. When their respective obligations are completed, a club runs smoothly. Specific tokens are used to symbolize the duties of each officer in the following installation service. Not only do the tokens represent the leadership positions of the club, but they serve to remind the officers of the pledge they make to their club to fulfill their responsibilities.

The gifts needed for this ceremony include a calculator for the treasurer, a box of stationery for the corresponding secretary, a pen for the secretary, a calendar for the second vice-president, a telephone/address book for the first vice-president, and a photo album for the president. The above items can be found at discount department stores, office supply stores, and gift stores. Make certain that you begin collecting the required items weeks in advance of the ceremony just in case you have a problem finding any of them. Cost for this idea depends on you. Most of the gifts come in high and low price ranges.

This lighthearted and brief ceremony is about 10 minutes in length and can be used for any organization, especially civic clubs whose officers would more than likely be able to use the gifts in their new offices. As stated earlier, shop early so that you have the necessary items in advance. Preparation of the script includes informing the new officers prior to the service that they will be required to answer an installation question with the words, "I do."

INSTALLATION CEREMONY

Officers of an organization have specific responsibilities. One takes care of the club's correspondence, another works with the program committee, and another appoints committees and chairmen. Although each officer does different tasks, it is the fulfillment of all of the officers' respective duties that keeps a club running efficiently.

Tonight, as the officers of the _____ (name of club) are installed, they will be given symbolic gifts. These tokens represent the officer's new obligations, and they serve to remind them of their promise to fulfill their new duties. Will the newly elected officers please come forward? (Have the officers line up in order with the treasurer first.)

The treasurer of a club collects dues, pays bills, balances the checkbook, and writes up monthly financial statements. As this club's new treasurer, do you promise to fulfill the duties of your office? (Officer should answer, "I do.")

Numbers play an important part in a treasurer's life. May this gift of a calculator assist you with your new responsibilities. (Give the gift to the officer.) Congratulations.

The corresponding secretary of a club writes notes, responds to letters, and promotes the image of a club. As this club's new corresponding secretary, do you promise to fulfill the duties of your office? (Officer should answer, "I do.")

Stationery is an important part of a corresponding secretary's life. May this note paper assist you with your new responsibilities. (Give the gift to the officer.) Congratulations.

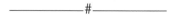

The secretary of a club takes minutes at every meeting, records the actions of a club, and keeps the club's historical records. As this club's new secretary, do you promise to fulfill the duties of your office? (Officer should answer, "I do.")

Writing is an important part of a secretary's life. May this pen assist you with your new responsibilities. (Give the gift to the officer.) Congratulations.

The second vice-president of a club chairs the program committee, helps in the selection of programs for the upcoming year, and assists the president. As this club's new second vice-president, do you promise to fulfill the duties of your office? (Officer should answer, "I do.")

Dates and times are an important part of a second vice-president's life. May this calendar assist you with your new responsibilities. (Give the gift to the officer.) Congratulations.

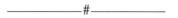

The first vice-president of a club chairs the membership committee, keeps all members, old and new, active and informed on club matters, and works closely with the president. As this club's new first vice-president, do you promise to fulfill the duties of your office? (Officer should answer, "I do.")

Phone numbers are important part of a first vice-president's life. May this telephone directory assist you with your new responsibilities. (Give the gift to the officer.) Congratulations.

The president of a club presides at meetings, appoints committees and chairmen, follows up on details, and represents the club at community functions. As this club's new president, do you promise to fulfill the duties of your office? (Officer should answer, "I do.")

You have been given the highest honor your club can bestow upon you. You will have many obligations, but should also have a great deal of fun. Pictures can preserve the memories of this hectic, but exciting, year for you. May this photo album serve as a reminder to you of your new responsibilities. (Give the gift to the officer.) Congratulations.

(To the membership.) Members, the officers of this club cannot work alone. You also have many tasks to perform. Supporting your club, you are called to remain active, work at club functions, and encourage your officers. The fulfillment of your obligations will ensure your club's success in accomplishing its goals.

Branching Out

Just as many different kinds of trees make up a forest, an organization is made up of various kinds of people. This ceremony uses the symbols of trees to indicate the distinctive duties of each office. Working together, the officers keep the club running smoothly. The officers are an integral part of the club leadership, just as trees are an important part of the forest.

A keepsake of the event would be to give each officer a potted seedling. The seedlings needed include a balsam fir for the treasurer, a weeping willow for the corresponding secretary, a white pine for the recording secretary, a white ash for the second vice-president, a sugar maple for the first vice-president, and a white oak for the president. Clay pots, potting soil, and seedlings should be purchased or found days prior to the ceremony. Once you have all the necessary items, transplant the seedlings into the pots and water them. Transplanting does not require much time, but finding the correct seedlings might, so do not wait until the last minute. Cost for this ceremony depends on the price of the seedlings. Clay pots and soil are fairly inexpensive. The trees mentioned above do not grow in all of the garden zones. These trees are primarily found east of the Mississippi River in North America. If you live in a region that does not have these trees, select one of the other gift ideas.

You might prefer to make a donation for the planting of a tree within your community in honor of the new officers. Make arrangements to find a location and have the officers select what type of tree to plant.

As a token, give each officer a certificate. A small picture of the appropriate tree should be placed on each officer's certificate. Use the same trees as listed in the above gift option. The certificates, which can be specialized by the use of a computer, should read as follows, " _____ (name of officer), to commemorate this day, a tree has been planted in your honor. As the new _____ (name of office) of the _____ (name of club), may you flourish and grow during your term of office." Date the certificate and sign it. Once the tree is planted, it would be nice to take a picture of the officers with their tree. Have reprints made up of the picture and mail one to each officer. The price range for this suggestion will vary depending on the type of tree selected.

A third alternative is to give each officer a book on trees. Larger coffee table books would be nice, but any book about trees could be used as long it contains the trees mentioned in the ceremony. The trees include a balsam fir, a weeping willow, a white pine, a white ash, a sugar maple, and a white oak. Before the ceremony, prepare each book by placing a bookmark between the pages mentioning the tree that corresponds to each officer. When an officer is installed, the book can be opened to the appropriate page which makes the gift a symbolic one. Remember, books might need to be ordered, so do not wait until the last minute. This suggestion requires time to go to a bookstore and time to prepare each book before the ceremony. It has the possibility of being expensive.

The following ceremony will last about 10 to 15 minutes. It is a solemn ceremony which could be used for any club, but is best suited for an environmental or garden club. Make certain the script and gifts are prepared in advance. In preparing the script, if the second or third gift idea is used, the words in parenthesis (symbol of a) are said during the installation since the actual seedling is not going to be given. Also, if a tree is donated in honor of the new officers, add that paragraph to the script.

INSTALLATION CEREMONY

Forests are made up of many different types of trees just as clubs are comprised of different types of members. Some trees make excellent shade trees, some are prized for their lumber, and others provide food for wildlife; but when put together, they become a forest.

Club officers also have different duties to perform. One will pay bills, one will take minutes, and another will preside at all club meetings. Like individual trees, each office has certain attributes, but when put together, they make a club run smoothly.

National forests and parks have been created with the sole purpose of safeguarding trees for future generations. Likewise, the newly elected officers are a valuable commodity to your club. They have been entrusted to safeguard the future of this club.

Tonight, the officers of the _____ (name of club) will be installed using a theme of trees. Will the newly elected officers please come forward? (Have the officers line up in order with the treasurer first.)

(To be read if the second gift option is selected: As the officers are installed tonight, they will be given certificates. Instead of receiving installation mementos, a tree is to be planted in their honor within the community.)

The treasurer is responsible for the club's finances. Time will be spent counting and depositing money, writing checks, balancing the checkbook, and keeping a detailed financial record for your club. Your job will require preciseness.

A (symbol of a) balsam fir is your gift to remind you of your new tasks. (Give the officer the gift, or the certificate.) The Balsam Fir can be recognized by its smooth, even cones, and its distinctive, fresh fragrance. Like the fir, may your records always be recognized by their even, exact, and up to date content. Congratulations and best wishes.

————————#————————

The corresponding secretary is responsible for the club's correspondence. Letters and notes will be written in reference to club matters, and a good club image must be projected to the community. Your job will require diplomacy.

A (symbol of a) weeping willow is your gift to remind you of your new tasks. (Give the officer the gift, or the certificate.) This flowing tree is known to flourish and grow in moist soil. It also easily propagates from stem cuttings. Like the willow, may your correspondence flow easily. Your writings should always help your organization flourish and grow by sparking the interest of others to join your club. Congratulations and best wishes.

The secretary is responsible for the club's historical records. Accurate minutes of the actions of your club must be taken at every meeting. These records are kept for reference, as well as historical significance. At any given time, an action of a previous meeting should be easily accessible. Your job will require accuracy.

A (symbol of a) white pine is your gift to remind you of your new tasks. (Give the officer the gift, or the certificate.) This tree with its long, soft, blue-green needles is greatly valued for its lumber. Like the pine, your minutes will be greatly valued and will become a part of your club's long history. Congratulations and best wishes.

The second vice-president is responsible for the club's program committee as well as being an assistant to the president. As chairman of the program committee, it is important to help your committee select educational, informative, and entertaining programs. Keep the programs varied, just as your membership's interests are varied. Be available to support and help your president. Your job will require flexibility.

A (symbol of a) white ash is your gift to remind you of your new tasks. (Give the officer the gift, or the certificate.) The ash is a tall tree prized for its tough, elastic wood. It can often be found growing in forests with oaks and maples. Like the ash, may your committee's programs be prized for their variety. Be flexible, just as the wood of the ash is. Congratulations and best wishes.

The first vice-president is responsible for the club's membership committee as well as being the right hand of the president. As chairman of the membership committee, it is important to keep all members, old and new, interested in club projects, and events. Invent ways to keep enthusiasm high. It is also important to support your president. Work closely with her, be available to her, and help her meet club goals. Your job will require perseverance.

A (symbol of a) sugar maple is your gift to remind you of your new tasks. (Give the officer the gift, or the certificate.) After oaks, the maple tree is the most familiar broad-leaf tree. From its sugary sap, many maple syrup and sugar products are made. Like the maple, you will be the highest officer after the president. It is your goal to keep all members focused on club matters. The by-product of members working together can be sweet, just like the sweet by-products of a sugar maple. Congratulations and best wishes.

The president is responsible for the leadership of the club. Your duties will include presiding at all club meetings, appointing chairmen and committees, following up on club matters, and representing your club at all functions. Your job will require patience and love.

A (symbol of a) white oak is your gift to remind you of your new tasks. (Give the officer the gift, or the certificate.) Oaks are considered to be the world's most important trees. They symbolize strength. The white oak is the most commonly known of the oaks, and it is prized for its lumber. Like the oak, you are your club's most important member and have been given your club's highest honor. May the oak help you find the strength needed to serve your club in this esteemed capacity. Congratulations and best wishes.

——————#——————

The officers of the _____ (name of club) have now been installed. However, they are only a small part of this club, just as each tree is only a small part of a forest. (To the membership.) Members, you are the rest of the forest in which these officers have just been planted. Your attributes combined with theirs make this club complete. Support one another, and you will grow together and have a very productive year.

Gift Index

Baseball cap, 53
Blocks, 7
Bookmarks, 57, 88, 106
Bottle of aspirin, 53
Bottles of glue, 53
Books, 53, 88, 103 106, 120
Calculator, 115
Calendar, 115
Candles, 17
Candy, 21
Cassette tapes, 12
Chain, pieces, 25
Copies of music, 67, 68
Decks of cards, 34
Eraser, 53
Flower seed packages, 43
Flowers, 13, 29, 43, 110
Fruit baskets, 48

Fruit, canned, 48
Fruit, dried, 48
Herb markers, 63
Herbs, 62
Herbs, dried, 62
Jigsaw puzzles, 72
Joke book, 53
Key chains, 76
Keys, 76
Kites, 80
Letter openers, 84
M
Magnets, 39
Measuring cups, 102
Measuring spoons, 102
Monetary donation, 119
Note cards, 44
Pens, 93, 115
Photo album, 115

Pictures, 39, 97
Pins, 57
Plants, 13, 62, 110
Plaques, 97, 106
Play money, 53
Posters, 39
Recipes, 102
Rubber pencil, 53
Sheet music, 12, 67
Shoes, 110
Stationery, 98, 115
Sun catchers, 30
Telephone/address book, 115
Tree seedlings, 119

Organization Index

Although most of the installation services can be used by any organization, the following index offers helpful suggestions in matching specific ceremonies with suitable clubs.

Civic or service, 17, 25, 34, 110, 115
Educational, 7, 72, 80, 84, 88
Garden, 43, 48, 62, 119
Historical, 84, 93, 97
Literary, 88, 93, 97, 102
Musical, 12, 67
Men's, 25, 53, 76, 84, 93
Nature, or environmental, 39, 43, 48, 62, 119
Religious, 17, 67, 84, 88, 106
Sports and leisure, 34, 72, 80
Students and teenagers, 21, 29, 57, 76, 80, 110
Theatrical, 12
Women's, 17, 29, 43, 57, 102, 110

Bibliography

Academic American Encyclopedia. 21 vols. Danbury, CT: Grolier Incorporated, 1991.

Bahr, Lauren S., ed. director. *Collier's Encyclopedia*, ed. in chief, Bernard Johnston. 24 vols. New York: P.F. Collier, Inc., 1993.'

Bartlett, John. *Familiar Quotations.* 15th edition. Boston: Little, Brown and Company, 1980.

Bock, Fred, gen. ed. *Hymns for the Family of God.* Nashville, TN: Paragon Associates, Inc., 1976.

Bremness, Lesley. *The Complete Book of Herbs.* New York: Viking Studio Books, 1988.

Clark, Linda. *The Ancient Art of Color Therapy.* Old Greenwich, CT: The Dean Adair Co., 1978.

Compton's Encyclopedia & Fact Index. 26 vols. Chicago: Compton's Learning Company, 1994.

Crowell, Robert L. *The Lore and Legends of Flowers.* New York: Thomas Y. Crowell, 1982.

Dupuis, Jean. *Marvellous World of Trees.* Translated by David Macrae. London: Abbey Library, 1976.

The Good News Bible. New York: American Bible Society, 1976.

Guralnik, David B., ed. in chief. *Webster's New World Dictionary of the American Language.* New York: The World Publishing Company, 1970.

Haslam, Gillian. *The Herbal Yearbook.* Surrey, England: Colour Library Books, Ltd., 1993.

Hill, Lewis. *Fruits and Berries for the Home Garden,* Pownal, VT: Garden Way Publishing, 1977.

Kadans, Dr. Joseph M. *Encyclopedia of Fruits, Vegetables, Nuts, and Seeds.* West Nyack, NY: Parker Publishing Company, Inc., 1973.

Leemy, Joseph. *Games & Fun with Playing Cards.* New York: Dover Publications, Inc., 1980.

Martin, Laura C. *Garden Flower Folklore.* Chester, CT: The Globe Pequot Press, 1987.

The Oxford Dictionary of Quotations. 3rd edition, reprinted with corrections. Oxford: Oxford University Press, 1980.

Schumann, Walter. *Gemstones of the World.* New York: Sterling Publishers Co., Inc., 1977.

The World Book Encyclopedia. 22 vols. Chicago: World Book, Inc., 1995.

Zim, Herbert S. and Alexander C. Martin. *Trees: A Guide to Familiar American Trees.* New York: Golden Press, 1956.

Dedication

I would like to dedicate this book to God who gave us the Word.

About the Author

A free-lance writer, Pat Hines has been writing news features for "The New Castle News" and "The South County News" since 1992. She is also the Children's Choir director at her church and has written choir music for the children to sing. One of her works, a children's Christmas musical, is scheduled for publication in 1998.

An active volunteer, Hines is involved with the General Federation of Women's Clubs, the American Cancer Society, the Girl Scouts of America, Meals on Wheels, Calvin Presbyterian Church, community theater, and various other local organizations. She is a graduate of Maryville College in Maryville, Tennessee, and currently resides in Ellwood City, Pennsylvania with her husband and two children.

Available from Brighton Publications, Inc.

Meeting Room Games: Getting Things Done in Committees by Nan Booth

Christmas Party Celebrations: 71 New & Exciting Plans for Holiday Fun by Denise Distel Dytrych

Folding Table Napkins: A New Look at a Traditional Craft by Sharon Dlugosch

Table Setting Guide by Sharon Dlugosch

Tabletop Vignettes by Sharon Dlugosch

Reunions for Fun-Loving Families by Nancy Funke Bagley

Games for Party Fun by Sharon Dlugosch

Romantic At-Home Dinners: Sneaky Strategies for Couples with Kids by Nan Booth/Gary Fischler

Kid-Tastic Birthday Parties: The Complete Party Planner for Today's Kids by Jane Chase

Games for Baby Shower Fun by Sharon Dlugosch

Baby Shower Fun by Sharon Dlugosch

An Anniversary to Remember: Years One to Seventy-Five by Cynthia Lueck Sowden

Games for Wedding Shower Fun by Sharon Dlugosch, Florence Nelson

Wedding Plans: 50 Unique Themes for the Wedding of Your Dreams by Sharon Dlugosch

Wedding Hints & Reminders by Sharon Dlugosch

Wedding Occasions: 101 New Party Themes for Wedding Showers, Rehearsal Dinners, Engagement Parties, and More! by Cynthia Lueck Sowden

Dream Weddings Do Come True: How to Plan a Stress-free Wedding by Cynthia Kreuger

Don't Slurp Your Soup: A Basic Guide to Business Etiquette by Elizabeth Craig

Hit the Ground Running: Communicate Your Way to Business Success by Cynthia Kreuger

These books are available in selected stores and catalogs. If you're having trouble finding them in your area, send a self-addressed, stamped, business-size envelope or call to request ordering information:

Brighton Publications, Inc.
P.O. Box 120706
St. Paul, MN 55112-0706

1-800-536-BOOK   http://www.partybooks.com